RECONSTRUCTING EVANGELICALISM

RECONSTRUCTING EVANGELICALISM

CHALLENGES AND OPPORTUNITIES

GERALD HIESTAND *and*
JOEL LAWRENCE, *editors*

CASCADE *Books* • Eugene, Oregon

RECONSTRUCTING EVANGELICALISM
Challenges and Opportunities

The Center for Pastor Theologians Series

Copyright © 2024 Wipf and Stock Publishers. All rights reserved. Except for brief quotations in critical publications or reviews, no part of this book may be reproduced in any manner without prior written permission from the publisher. Write: Permissions, Wipf and Stock Publishers, 199 W. 8th Ave., Suite 3, Eugene, OR 97401.

Cascade Books
An Imprint of Wipf and Stock Publishers
199 W. 8th Ave., Suite 3
Eugene, OR 97401

www.wipfandstock.com

PAPERBACK ISBN: 978-1-6667-8967-6
HARDCOVER ISBN: 978-1-6667-8968-3
EBOOK ISBN: 978-1-6667-8969-0

Cataloguing-in-Publication data:

Names: Hiestand, Gerald, 1974–, editor. | Lawrence, Joel, editor.

Title: Reconstructing evangelicalism : challenges and opportunities / edited by Gerald Hiestand and Joel Lawrence.

Description: Eugene, OR : Cascade Books, 2024 | Series: The Center for Pastor Theologians Series | Includes bibliographical references and index.

Identifiers: ISBN 978-1-6667-8967-6 (paperback) | ISBN 978-1-6667-8968-3 (hardcover) | ISBN 978-1-6667-8969-0 (ebook)

Subjects: LCSH: Evangelicalism.

Classification: BR1640 .R33 2024 (paperback) | BR1640 .R33 (ebook)

12/20/24

To the Ecclesial Fellows of the Center for Pastor Theologians, who are pursuing God's calling to faithfully shepherd the church in these challenging days. Thank you for your commitment to the church, theology, and pastoral ministry.

Contents

Permissions | ix

Acknowledgments | xi

Introduction: The Challenges and Opportunities of Reconstructing Evangelicalism | xiii
  —Gerald Hiestand and Joel Lawrence

Part One: Challenges

1. Imagining a New Reformation: The Babylonian Captivity of the Evangelical Church | 3
   —Karen Swallow Prior

2. A Call for Prophetic Leadership: The Church's Recipe for Responding to White Christian Nationalism and the Great Replacement Theory | 16
   —Jonathan C. Augustine

3. In Search of Disciples of Christ | 30
   —Elizabeth Conde-Frazier

4 In Search of "Biblical" Masculinity: Today's Crisis of Masculinity | 42
—Zachary Wagner

5 Evangelicalism in Nigeria: A Bowl of Mixed Fruits | 55
—Babatunde Oladimeji

Part Two: Opportunities

6 The Gospel According to John (Webster): Toward an Evangelical Evangelical Theology | 73
—Kevin J. Vanhoozer

7 Seeing the World through Bavinckian Eyes | 88
—Gayle Doornbos

8 Mission After Evangelicalism | 102
—Michael Niebauer

9 How Church History Can Help Us Reconstruct Evangelicalism | 116
—Gavin Ortlund

10 The End of the Gospel: Refocusing Our "Why" as a Wesleyan Contribution to Reconstructing Evangelicalism | 126
—Matt O'Reilly

11 Reconstructing an Architecture for Evangelical Cultural Interaction | 139
—Walter Kim

Index | 153

Permissions

Scripture quotations marked (ESV) are from the ESV® Bible (The Holy Bible, English Standard Version®), © 2001 by Crossway, a publishing ministry of Good News Publishers. Used by permission. All rights reserved. The ESV text may not be quoted in any publication made available to the public by a Creative Commons license. The ESV may not be translated in whole or in part into any other language.

Scripture quotations marked (NASB) are taken from the (NASB®) New American Standard Bible®, Copyright © 1960, 1971, 1977, 1995, 2020 by The Lockman Foundation. Used by permission. All rights reserved. www.lockman.org.

Scripture quotations marked (NIV) are taken from the Holy Bible, New International Version®, NIV®. Copyright © 1973, 1978, 1984, 2011 by Biblica, Inc.™ Used by permission of Zondervan. All rights reserved worldwide. www.zondervan.com. The "NIV" and "New International Version" are trademarks registered in the United States Patent and Trademark Office by Biblica, Inc.™

Scripture quotations marked (NRSV) are taken from the New Revised Standard Version Bible, copyright © 1989 National Council of the Churches of Christ in the United States of America. Used by permission. All rights reserved worldwide.

PERMISSIONS

Scripture quotations marked (NET) are from the NET Bible.® https://netbible.com. Copyright ©1996, 2019. Used with permission from Biblical Studies Press, L.L.C. All rights reserved.

Scripture quotations marked (KJV) are from The Authorized (King James) Version. Rights in the Authorized Version in the United Kingdom are vested in the Crown. Reproduced by permission of the Crown's patentee, Cambridge University Press.

"Imagining a New Reformation: The Babylonian Captivity of the Evangelical Church" is adapted from material in *The Evangelical Imagination* by Karen Swallow Prior. Copyright © 2023. Used by permission of Brazos Press, a division of Baker Publishing Group.

Acknowledgments

As IN THE PAST, we owe a debt of gratitude to the contributors of this volume. The subject of reconstructing Evangelicalism is a challenging one, and we are grateful to the men and women who have helped us to think more deeply about the challenges and opportunities before us.

Likewise, we are grateful to the Center for Pastor Theologians (CPT), the organizer of the conference from which the papers of this book are drawn. The Center has served as a catalyst for our work and has been a repository of wisdom and counsel on all things pastoral and theological. The staff of the Center—Todd Wilson (president until October 2023), Joel Lawrence (executive director until 2023, and now president), Rae Paul (director of operations), and Zach Wagner (director of programs)—did a tremendous job organizing the conference, and we deeply value their ongoing work on behalf of the mission and vision of the CPT.

In the same spirit, we are deeply grateful for the partnership of the CPT's five senior theological mentors: Scott Hafemann, Doug Sweeney, Peter Leithart, Kevin Vanhoozer, and Timothy George. Their commitment to the CPT's mission, their contribution to the Fellowships, and their friendship and encouragement to the two of us have been an important catalyst for the CPT project and its associated publications.

Likewise, we continue to be grateful for Calvary Memorial Church in Oak Park, Illinois, the congregation where CPT co-founders Todd Wilson

ACKNOWLEDGMENTS

and Gerald Hiestand have been privileged to serve as pastors. Calvary has graciously served as the host home for the CPT for more than a decade, and it is not an overstatement to say that the CPT would not be what it is without Calvary's partnership and support. The use of Calvary's building, the help from Calvary's staff, and the support of Calvary's elder council has been a tremendous resource for the CPT.

And finally, we owe Myndi Lawrence and Seth Porch a special debt of gratitude for their labors as copy and production editors for this volume. Myndi did a tremendous job in organizing and communicating with the contributors, and Seth did a great job finalizing the book by editing, chasing down missing citations, and indexing, in order to produce a completed manuscript ready for submission.

Introduction

The Challenges and Opportunities of Reconstructing Evangelicalism

IN OCTOBER OF 2022, the Center for Pastor Theologians (CPT) gathered a community of pastors, ministry leaders, and theological educators to engage the question of the past, present, and future of Evangelicalism.

This was the seventh CPT national conference. Our purpose in hosting these conferences is to bring people together from across the evangelical spectrum to interact with a range of thinkers, most from within that spectrum and some from outside it. In our polarized age, gatherings of this kind are increasingly rare. More and more, Christians are following the pattern of the broader culture and moving into self-affirming echo chambers. As an organization, we want to counteract this movement and establish spaces where pastor theologians can step into a theologically challenging, relationally rich, and ecumenically diverse communion.

The 2022 conference came at a time of deep questioning by many in our culture about the viability of Evangelicalism and about the accommodation of the evangelical movement to the varied political and cultural passions in America. Over the past few years, Evangelicalism has been marked by a deconstructionist movement in which many, especially younger, Evangelicals have been leaving the evangelical tradition. Some have left the Christian faith altogether due to what they perceive to be deep inconsistencies, inadequacies, and hypocrisies. The ongoing deconstruction in the church and culture has focused on such topics as evangelical theology, approaches to politics, public witness, human sexuality, gender, biblical interpretation, and racial injustice.

In setting the theme of the conference, significant questions were raised: What is Evangelicalism? What is the nature of the challenges facing the evangelical movement in the late modern world? Is deconstruction a necessary part of the church's commitment to always be reforming, or is it driven by cultural accommodation that evangelical leaders would do well to resist? Does moving too quickly to discuss reconstruction signal a lack of seriousness in grappling with the challenges facing Evangelicalism? What can American Evangelicalism learn from the global evangelical tradition, a community that isn't facing the same questions of deconstruction that we are in the West?

Bringing together pastors and other ministry leaders who approach questions from different perspectives on the theological spectrum made for a time of rich dialogue, the energy of which is captured in this volume. The volume is divided into two parts: Part 1: Challenges and Part 2: Opportunities. As Evangelicals, we believe in both the fallenness of humanity as well as the hope of resurrection. As those who believe in human sinfulness, it should come as no surprise that we, and the institutions we form, would be marred by human frailty and fallenness. At the same time, acknowledging our sinfulness must move us toward the grace of transformation as we seek the renewing work of the Spirit among us.

As such, this volume's structure is itself a reflection of evangelical commitments. It is our hope and prayer that this collection of papers will call readers to grapple with challenges and seek opportunities. We are convinced that if the evangelical movement is to both accurately assess the condition of Evangelicalism as we enter the mid-twenty-first century and encourage Evangelicalism toward a deeper reflection of the gospel and character of Christ, it is critical to have the courage to step into places of challenge, while also searching for the opportunities being opened by the Spirit.

Dr. Gerald Hiestand
Senior Pastor, Calvary Memorial Church, Oak Park, Illinois
Co-founder and Board Chair, Center for Pastor Theologians

Dr. Joel Lawrence
President, Center for Pastor Theologians

Contributors

JONATHAN C. AUGUSTINE (JD, Tulane University; DMin, Duke University) serves as senior pastor of St. Joseph AME Church in Durham, North Carolina, and as a member of the consulting faculty at Duke Divinity School. He is the author of *When Prophets Preach: Leadership and the Politics of the Pulpit* (Fortress, 2023) and *Called to Reconciliation: How the Church Can Model Justice, Diversity and Inclusion* (Baker Academic, 2022).

ELIZABETH CONDE-FRAZIER (PhD, Boston College) is a practical theologian and an ordained pastor of the American Baptist Churches. She is currently the director of the Association for Hispanic Theological Education. She is the author of *Atando Cabos: Latinx Contributions to Theological Education* (Eerdmans, 2021) and co-author of *A Many Colored Kingdom: Multicultural Dynamics for Spiritual Formation* (Baker, 2004) and *Latina Evangélicas: A Theological Survey from the Margins* (Wipf and Stock, 2013).

GAYLE DOORNBOS (PhD, University of St. Michael's College) is an associate professor of theology at Dordt University. She has contributed to multiple journals and edited volumes, including the entry on D. H. Th. Vollenhoven in the *T&T Clark Handbook of Neo-Calvinism* and "Bavinck's Doctrine of God: Absolute, Divine Personality" in the *Journal of Biblical and Theological Studies*.

CONTRIBUTORS

WALTER KIM (PhD, Harvard University) is the president of the National Association of Evangelicals. He previously served as a pastor at Boston's Park Street Church and at churches in Vancouver, Canada, and Charlottesville, Virginia, as well as a campus chaplain at Yale University. He serves on the boards of Christianity Today and World Relief and consults with a wide range of organizations.

MICHAEL NIEBAUER (PhD, Duquesne University) is an Anglican pastor and the director of Heritage Mission. He has contributed articles to multiple academic journals and is the author of *Virtuous Persuasion: A Theology of Christian Mission* (Lexham, 2022).

BABATUNDE OLADIMEJI (PhD, DMin, Asbury Theological Seminary) is a priest of the Diocese of Kebbi, Church of Nigeria (Anglican Communion), and currently serves as the senior pastor of Chadron United Methodist Church in Chadron, Nebraska. He teaches, coaches, and consults for organizations both in the United States and internationally. He has contributed to multiple journals and books, including "A History of Charismatic Influence on the Anglican Church in Nigeria" in *Journal of Religion and Society in Africa*, and "Servant Leadership in John 13:1–14: A Reflection on Professor Dapo Asaju's Transformational Leadership Style" in *Dearth of Integrity: The Bane of Leadership in Nigeria*, edited by Selome Kuponu (Lagos State University, 2021)

MATT O'REILLY (PhD, University of Gloucestershire) is lead pastor at Hope Hull United Methodist Church near Montgomery, Alabama, and director of research at Wesley Biblical Seminary. He is the author of *Paul and the Resurrected Body: Social Identity and Ethical Practice* (SBL, 2020).

GAVIN ORTLUND (PhD, Fuller Theological Seminary) is the president of *Truth Unites* and theologian-in-residence at Immanuel Nashville in Nashville, Tennessee. He is the author of numerous books, including *Humility: The Joy of Self-Forgetfulness* (Crossway, 2023), *Why God Makes Sense in a World that Doesn't: The Beauty of Christian Theism* (Baker Academic, 2021), *Augustine's Doctrine of Creation: Ancient Wisdom for Current Controversy* (IVP Academic, 2020), and *Anselm's Pursuit of Joy: A Commentary on the* Proslogion (Catholic University of America Press, 2020).

KAREN SWALLOW PRIOR (PhD, State University of New York at Buffalo) is an independent scholar, opinion columnist at *Religion News Service*, and author of *The Evangelical Imagination: How Stories, Images, and Metaphors Created a*

CONTRIBUTORS

Culture in Crisis (Brazos, 2023) and *On Reading Well: Finding the Good Life in Great Books* (Brazos, 2018).

KEVIN J. VANHOOZER (PhD, Cambridge University) is research professor of systematic theology at Trinity Evangelical Divinity School. He has also taught at the University of Edinburgh and the Wheaton College Graduate School. He is the author of *The Drama of Doctrine: A Canonical Linguistic Approach to Christian Theology* (WJK, 2005) and *Pictures at a Theological Exhibition: Scenes of the Church's Worship, Witness, and Wisdom* (IVP, 2016).

ZACHARY WAGNER (MSt, University of Oxford) is a New Testament DPhil candidate at Keble College, University of Oxford. He is an ordained minister and serves as the director of programs at the Center for Pastor Theologians. He is the author of *Non-Toxic Masculinity: Recovering Healthy Male Sexuality* (IVP, 2023).

Part One

CHALLENGES

1

Imagining a New Reformation

The Babylonian Captivity of the Evangelical Church

KAREN SWALLOW PRIOR

INTRODUCTION

ABOUT A CENTURY BEFORE the Protestant Reformation, Geoffrey Chaucer wrote *The Canterbury Tales*. This unfinished collection of stories revolves around a group of mostly strangers—who collectively represent the three medieval classes or estates (nobility, clergy, and layperson)—riding horseback on an obligatory pilgrimage to the cathedral at Canterbury. To pass the time along the way, they hold a storytelling contest. Before they begin, we are introduced to each pilgrim in the general prologue.[1] Each pilgrim's physical appearance also reveals his or her moral character, in keeping with the medieval belief in physiognomy, a personality assessment based on one's outer appearance. The pilgrims are also introduced in order of decreasing moral character. The last—and therefore most immoral character on the pilgrimage—is the Pardoner.

In the medieval church, pardoners were laypeople, essentially clerks who carried out the function of raising money for the church by selling indulgences—or pardons—for sins. Pardons were substitutes for penance. While pardons were officially sanctioned by the church, those who trafficked in them often exploited the office for personal gain.

---

1. Chaucer, "General Prologue," in *Canterbury Tales*, 23–36.

In the prologue to his tale, the Pardoner tells the other pilgrims that his tale will consist of the one sermon he delivers wherever he goes to peddle his wares.[2] He may have only one sermon, but it is so well-practiced that it forms, arguably, the most moral and artistically perfect tale of all in *The Canterbury Tales*.[3] Ironically, given the Pardoner's ignoble character, his story exemplifies the moral lesson that the root of evil is greed (based on the common Latin phrase *radix malorum est cupiditas*).

But before he tells his amazing tale, the Pardoner confesses (really, brags) openly and unashamedly to the other pilgrims what he is up to. He tells them that he travels from town to town, delivers this sermon on greed, and uses the guilt it conjures in his listeners to swindle them into buying his indulgences or the alleged magical powers of the fake relics he also carries with him. He openly makes this confession, but it does not stop him from trying to swindle the other pilgrims at the conclusion of his tale. The pilgrims do not fall for it. But what is most interesting and revealing is that the Pardoner is seduced and deluded by his own rhetorical powers. He believes he is so good that he can tell his audience what he is up to and still convince them to be swayed by the power of his story. He has fooled countless victims along the way (so perhaps we cannot blame him for his confidence). But this is the kind of rampant corruption in the church that Chaucer's tale exposes. A century before the Reformation, Chaucer—a middle-class public servant, clerk, and poet—saw and powerfully illustrated the need for church reform.

A Babylonian Captivity

The original aim of what came to be called the Protestant Reformation was not to breach but to reform the existing institution. But rather than face the truth about the church's egregious departures from the doctrines taught in Scripture, the leaders in Rome, Martin Luther complained, "protected themselves by these walls in such a way that no one has been able to reform them." Because of their self-protection, he lamented, "the whole of Christendom has fallen abominably."[4]

Upon refusing to recant some of his key criticisms of the church, Luther was excommunicated by Pope Leo X in 1521. Luther was left no choice but to form a church body that would better reflect the Scriptures he had long studied and that, he saw, the church had abandoned. Other Reformers across

---

2. Chaucer, "Pardoner's Prologue," in *Canterbury Tales*, 194–96.
3. Chaucer, "Pardoner's Tale," in *Canterbury Tales*, 196–202.
4. Luther, "To the Christian Nobility," 126.

Europe followed suit, and what followed was a range of reforms that attempted to restore and uphold the councils and creeds established in the first centuries of the church and make them manifest.

The Protestant Reformation was centered on truth—the truth of biblical doctrine. Yes, the medieval church's widespread corruption took the form of practices, but these evil deeds—including the sale of pardons and indulgences for sin that expanded the church's wealth and power to obscene levels by taking advantage of the fact that the illiterate masses could not read the Bible for themselves—were made possible by distorting the truth. The church was able to get away with it because few could read the Bible for themselves and thereby see the lies. The people—who had no political power and no ability to read the Bible even if they were able to gain access to one—were made captive by illiteracy to an institution that grew more corrupt as it grew wealthier and more powerful.

What holds Evangelicals—who not only can read but have easy access to Bibles of all kinds—captive today? That is an important question.

Captive Evangelicalism

One answer is that we suffer under a different kind of illiteracy today, another kind of "dark age" created by too much information, too much disinformation and misinformation, and an inability (or unwillingness) to do the labor necessary to "read" information, the times, and ourselves better. Perhaps this kind of functional illiteracy is a crisis of the imagination.

I do not mean just our individual imaginative capacities (although surely that forms part of the current crisis). What I mean is that we are in the midst of a crisis that has emerged from the deformities of our communal stories, metaphors, and images.

Collectively, the works of our imaginations reflect and create cultures. Sculptures uphold standards of beauty. Love songs shape our views of romantic love. Movies give us images of sexual encounters that establish new norms and expectations. "Poets," as Percy Bysshe Shelley famously wrote in 1821, "are the unacknowledged legislators of the world."[5]

While the work of imagination contributes to the making of a culture, a culture in turn provides individuals with a precognitive framework—a framework that includes unconscious, unarticulated, and unstated underlying assumptions—that directs, shapes, and forms our thoughts and desires and imaginations in ways we do not necessarily recognize. Think of the unseen

---

5. Shelley, *Defence of Poetry*, 90.

parts that form the structure of a house. Philosopher Charles Taylor calls these frameworks "social imaginaries." In his early work, *Modern Social Imaginaries*, Taylor defines the social imaginary as a culture's shared pool of "images, stories, and legends" that shape one's social existence and expectations and "the deeper normative notions and images that underlie these expectations."[6] The social imaginary forms a "common understanding that enables us to carry out the collective practices that make up our social life." This "understanding is both factual and normative; that is, we have a sense of how things usually go, but this is interwoven with an idea of how they ought to go."[7] In other words, our social imaginary is both descriptive and prescriptive. It makes a particular practice possible, and, in turn, "it is the practice that largely carries the understanding" forward.[8] Our practices, Taylor says, both reflect and maintain "self-conceptions" and "modes of understanding."[9]

A culture is composed of both the ingredients we know and recognize—material artifacts, social and political relationships and institutions, and ideas and beliefs—and the unexpressed assumptions and attitudes that make up the social imaginaries therein. The autonomy and agency that the modern age has taught us to believe in (part of our social imaginary) fools us into ignoring the fact that we are shaped by the culture in which we exist in ways that can be difficult, if not impossible, to recognize.

Although there is no one Evangelicalism (only "Evangelicalisms"[10]), it is fair to say that the Evangelicalism that has greatly defined the American church (and America) in recent years has created a culture that has seemingly overwhelmed other contemporary cultures. Evangelicalism has its own imaginaries—the unexamined, precognitive assumptions, stories, images, and metaphors that give birth to beliefs, actions, and practices.

If Evangelicalism is a house, then these unexamined assumptions are its floor joists, wall studs, beams, and rafters—holding everything together but unseen, covered over by tile, paint, paper, and ceilings. What we do not see, we do not think about. Until something goes wrong and something needs replacement. Or restoration. Or reform.

The evangelical house is badly in need of repair. We must confess, with Augustine, about ourselves and our movement, "My soul's house is too meager

---

6. Taylor, *Modern Social Imaginaries*, 23.
7. Taylor, *Modern Social Imaginaries*, 24.
8. Taylor, *Modern Social Imaginaries*, 25.
9. Taylor, *Modern Social Imaginaries*, 31.
10. Du Mez, "There Are No Real Evangelicals."

for you to visit. It is falling down; rebuild it. Inside are things that would disgust you to see: I confess this, and I know it. But who's going to clean it?"[11]

The crisis facing American Evangelicalism today—manifest in increasing division, decreasing church membership and attendance, mounting revelations of abuse and cover-up of abuse, and an ongoing reckoning with our racist past and present—is one in which the decorative layers that have long adorned the evangelical house are being peeled away. Now we can see, some of us for the first time, the foundational parts of its structure. Some of these parts are solid. Some are rotten. Some can be salvaged. Some ought not to be saved.

Many have said that what has been exposed within the evangelical movement in recent days, months, and years is apocalyptic.

It is.

Uncovering Evangelicalism

The biblical meaning of the Greek word translated into English as "apocalypse" is simply an *uncovering* or *revelation*. We often associate apocalypse with the end of the world because of the vision given in the book of Revelation about future days. We also make this association because some moments of revelation in human, church, or personal history do seem like the end of the world. There are moments when this particular historical moment—which has included crises in the church, the first global pandemic in a century, and deep political polarization—seems to portend the end of the world. But perhaps it is only, as the rock group R.E.M. put it, "the end of the world as we know it."[12] And maybe that is fine.

Many truths that have been hidden are being brought to light. Many deeds that have been covered up are being uncovered. Many assumptions that have been unexamined are being brought to the surface and scrutinized in order that we may consider whether they are rooted in eternal truths or merely in human traditions. In the process, Jesus is revealing more of himself. As he said to his Father, "You have hidden these things from the wise and learned, and revealed them to little children" (Matt 11:25 NIV). It is significant that the word translated as "revealed" in this verse is the Greek word for "apocalypse."

Some of what is hidden from us is spiritual reality, divine truths that can be revealed to us only through God's divine power.

Some of what is hidden remains so because of our own limited human nature. The Pardoner's belief that he could be utterly transparent about his

---

11. Augustine, *Confessions* 1.6.
12. R.E.M., "It's the End."

corrupt ways and still get people to buy what he was selling—"I could stand in the middle of Fifth Avenue and shoot somebody, and I wouldn't lose any voters, OK?"[13]—expresses something uncomfortably true about the complexities of human nature. I cannot explain the psychological and spiritual psychoses behind this phenomenon. But I do want to try to examine the role our imaginations play and the power they have to shape the way we see, well, everything.

While the most literal understanding of the imagination centers on image-making—the recreation of pictures and sensations—language is inseparable from the working of the human imagination. Language allows humans to make connections that exceed the merely instinctual level of a mouse and a lever or Pavlov and his dogs. This is where metaphor comes in. A metaphor, simply put, is a similitude, the seeing of one thing in terms of another. "You are just a *vapor* that appears for a little while and then vanishes away" (Jas 4:14 NASB). "The Lord is my shepherd," Ps 23:1 proclaims. We know instantly what these metaphors are saying. And we know, too, that they are not to be understood literally. Metaphors are so prevalent that it is easy not to see them. All language is metaphorical, after all.

This hiddenness of the metaphorical nature of language contributes to a phenomenon that linguists call *hypocognition*. Hypocognition describes experiences and concepts that have little or no representation in words (whether in a particular language or within a culture), and therefore remain under-recognized, unarticulated, and even unseen. They fly under the radar, so to speak. Hypocognition involves not only concepts that are "accepted but unexamined," but also obscures what is left out. In short, hypocognition refers to the "unknown unknowns."[14]

To examine previously unexamined assumptions is to acknowledge not only that there are things we do not know—aspects of reality yet hidden to us—but there are also things we do not even know that we do not know.

Reforming Evangelicalism

To be clear, we do not want to conflate Evangelicalism with the Reformation. Not all of Protestantism is Evangelicalism (although sometimes it seems that way). In relation to the revolution wrought by the Protestant Reformation, the evangelical movement clearly is but a coda, an addendum. Yet, three hundred years after inking this postscript to the Reformation, Evangelicalism is in the midst of a reckoning. And I do not think it is overly presumptuous or

---

13. Diamond, "Trump," para. 2.
14. Wu and Dunning, "Unknown Unknowns."

self-aggrandizing as an Evangelical to suggest that as Evangelicalism goes (at least in the near future), so goes Protestantism. (We certainly saw that as a large swath of Evangelicalism went, so went the nation and much of the world.)

If the Reformation was over the word as written (over who can and should read and interpret it), then this reckoning of Evangelicalism concerns the Word as it has been incarnated. If the Reformation was over the truth revealed in Scripture, then this evangelical reckoning is over the way and the life revealed in Jesus—and how the church has failed to follow and embody it.

They—the word written and the Word incarnated—cannot be separated, of course. But the failure of the evangelical imagination is in failing to see and embody this whole. Instead, we have developed a false division between biblical theology and spiritual formation. Between orthodoxy and orthopraxy. Between religion and politics.[15] Jesus showed us the way to unite these—indeed, he was the union of these things.

Jesus said, "I am the way, and the truth, and the life" (John 14:6 NASB).

Consider what it means that Jesus calls himself "the life." Part of what has always defined the evangelical movement is its focus on the essential gospel message that through Jesus Christ—and through him alone—one gains eternal life. Evangelicals have tended to focus so much on getting to heaven, however, that the reason for existence in this earthly life is often elusive. Even more often forgotten is that eternal life will be spent here—in a new heaven and a new earth. Eternal life does not begin in the future. Eternal life begins *now*.

Jesus also says he is "the truth." Among the defining characteristics of Evangelicalism, the centrality of the Bible is prominent. Evangelicals have always emphasized biblical truth over church tradition (and over personal experience, at least theoretically and until more recently[16]). Even the spirit of activism that David Bebbington identifies as part of what defines Evangelicalism manifests in applying beliefs about biblical truth in a proactive way.[17] Eighteenth-century British Evangelicals were activists in abolishing the slave trade, promoting animal welfare, and reforming capital punishment and labor laws. In the nineteenth and twentieth centuries, Evangelicals became activists in education, voting, and temperance. The concerns may change, but the heart of Evangelicalism has always been application of what is understood to be biblical truth to the cultural issues of the day.

Jesus is also "the way." No Christian—and certainly no Evangelical—would deny it. But when Evangelicals talk about Jesus being "the way," it is

---

15. For a reading that reintegrates religion and politics, see Wright, "Paul and Caesar," 173–93.

16. See Trueman, *Rise and Triumph*.

17. Bebbington, *Evangelicalism in Modern Britain*, 10–12.

usually imagined in a straightforward, literal manner: Jesus is the way to God, the way to eternal life, the way to heaven. While this is true, there is so much more embedded in that word, in that image, than simply a path or a road (which is what the Greek word *hodos* in John 14:6 means).[18] Evangelicals tend to emphasize how Jesus is the way *to* something. But he is also the way, period. Consider the difference between saying, "This is the road into town" and "This is the road." One is a means to something. The other is something in and of itself. Jesus is not only a means to something. He is an ultimate end.

If the Reformation was a crisis of authority—one that rightly gave highest authority to the Bible rather than the priests—then this reckoning (or perhaps even a new reformation) is one of credibility: Do we who profess to believe in the authority of the word present ourselves as credible witnesses of that Way, that Truth, and that Life?

The foibles and faults of the church, while always reflecting the fallible and unchanging human condition of the people who comprise it, will inevitably reflect the particular limitations of its particular time and place. Christian leaders of churches in suburban Chicago in the twenty-first century are not as likely as those criticized by Geoffrey Chaucer in *The Canterbury Tales* to try to sell congregants the magical healing powers of a sheep's bone. Nor would the seventeenth-century Puritans have embraced a view of God that is reflected in today's prosperity gospel or moralistic therapeutic deism.[19] And most of us today are not going to use the Bible to support chattel slavery.

Like so many other movements, powers, and institutions over the course of human history, the evangelical empire that has reigned in America for so long is, by some measures, undergoing loss—loss of position, privilege, influence, and power. It is easy for those who have benefited from this empire (I count myself among these) to feel a sense of loss. Having something you have always had taken away is—at least by human calculations—a loss.

But imagine what might be gained.

When Jesus invites us to follow him, it means more than just walking behind him on the road toward a destination, or the cross serving as a plank placed over a chasm between you and God. Jesus invites us to adopt his way, and his ways. He invites us to be like him. To imitate him. To call his Father "Father," too. To die to self as he did. To participate in his nature. To be grafted onto the true vine in order to bear fruit that tastes like him—divine.

Some philosophers say that Jesus entered the world at the precise historical moment in which a convergence of Jewish history and Greek thought gave birth to modern consciousness, a time when the I AM who revealed himself

---

18. "John 14:6," NASB Lexicon, Bible Hub.
19. Smith and Denton, *Soul Searching*.

in the Old Testament became incarnated within a human culture ready to receive him and spread his message to all people.[20] Indeed, Jesus says "I am" quite a few times.

Some would even say that the birth of the modern individual—whose conscious existence begins with the expression "I am"—took place all the way back when Christ was born.

For example, it was not by mere accident, Marshall McLuhan says, that "Christianity began in the Greco-Roman culture." With the invention of the phonetic alphabet, the Greeks made it possible to have a "sense of private substantial identity—a self" that "is to this day utterly unknown" in other parts of the world. "Christianity was introduced into a matrix of culture in which the individual had enormous significance," claims McLuhan, a concept that was "not characteristic of other world cultures."[21] With literacy, God's people would have the ability to read longer texts of Scripture to "nurture a sense of divine presence that dwelt internally, in the heart and mind."[22]

This interior life is, of course, the site of the imagination.

God, who calls himself I AM, came to earth, united in spirit and flesh, fully human and fully divine, at just the right moment in human history when human language was ready to take a form that would awaken individual consciousness, interior life, and imagination in a way that would forever alter history and humanity. Conscience as we understand it today was introduced by Christianity. Each time we express ourselves beginning with the words, "I am . . ." we express consciousness, the inner life, and imagination in a way that reflects God's image in us.[23]

Among the most known and repeated words of Jesus are these from the instructions he gives his disciples upon sending them out: "Whoever finds their life will lose it, and whoever loses their life for my sake will find it" (Matt 10:39 NIV).

Perhaps we have heard and read these words so often that they have lost their meaning. Or perhaps we have heard and read these words so often within particular contexts that their meaning has shrunk. We might think it means only that we gain eternal life by surrendering our life to Jesus. It does mean that. We might think it means that we find ultimate meaning and purpose in life when we serve Jesus. It does. But maybe it also means more specific,

---

20. Vernon, *Secret History of Christianity*, 28–41.

21. McLuhan, "Electric Consciousness," 81.

22. Vernon, *Secret History of Christianity*, 27.

23. Mark Vernon and Malcolm Guite have done a lot of work exploring these ideas in detail. See, e.g., Vernon and Guite, "Faith of the Inklings"; Guite, "Evolving Consciousness"; Vernon, "Mossy Face of Christ."

concrete things in our particular lives and times. Maybe it means that when we lose platform, or position, or privilege, or pay, or authority, or respect, or work, or elections, or jobs, or followers, or friends, or health, or limbs, or ease, we might find more of our life in Christ.

This loss of language, of meaning—whether through overfamiliarity or lack of real familiarity in the first place—is, at heart, what I am hoping to help us recover in this chapter. What is imagination but an opening of the eyes of our hearts?

As Jesus said of many who were exposed to his parables, "Though seeing, they do not see; though hearing, they do not hear or understand" (Matt 13:13 NIV). We must ask Jesus to open our eyes and ears, to renew our imaginations. Indeed, Paul implores the Lord in Eph 1:18 to open the eyes of our hearts so that our hearts will be flooded with the light of his truth.

Seeing is hard.

Change is hard.

But change (for us fallible humans in this fallen world) is also inevitable.

Change is good: *semper reformanda* (always reforming).

The complete phrase from which this oft-repeated refrain comes—*ecclesia reformata, semper reformanda* (the church reformed, always reforming)—emerged following the Protestant Reformation. It expressed the idea that while the church had been reformed in light of the grievous errors that had festered for so long in the church, reforming must also be an ongoing process, not only for each individual believer through the process of sanctification, but for the church itself.

The root of *reformation is formation*.

Formation speaks of the Way. The way of salvation. The way of living. The way of growing. The way of going.

The church cannot rest on her laurels. Even the church *reformed* continues to need *reforming*.

Is the church in a 500-year moment? Will the reckoning lead to a new reformation? This is an important question.

In one of the last essays he wrote before his assassination in 1968, Martin Luther King, Jr. reflected on that quintessential American tale of Rip Van Winkle who climbed up a mountain and slept for twenty years. King observes, "The most striking thing about this story is not that Rip Van Winkle slept twenty years, but that he slept through a revolution that would alter the course of human history."[24]

We need an Awakening. A Greater Awakening.

---

24. King, *Where Do We Go From Here?*, 181.

Awakening Evangelicalism

Whether in the Bible, in ancient myth, in modern psychology, or in common parlance, the metaphor of awakening suggests some moment of illumination or enlightenment that leads to change. So while the metaphor of awakening is not distinctively evangelical, or even distinctively Christian, it has been central to the evangelical imagination since the movement's beginnings. This fact is expressed no more obviously than in the name given to the series of revivals in America known as the Great Awakenings. The Evangelical Revival of the early eighteenth century occurred out of a sense that the church in both England and America had, two centuries after the Reformation, fallen back asleep. In America, the first Great Awakening was foreseen in the inchoate visions of human equality and progress that eventually came to be called the American Dream. Both the Dream and the Awakening are more than mere facts of history. They are the outworking of a collective imagination.

Scholars characterize awakenings in general as extended times of revitalization in which values and beliefs undergo deep examination and change.[25] In contemporary culture, we speak often of pricking or awakening the conscience, whether in matters of personal, individual sin or of social, systemic wrongs.

The concept of conscience which early Christianity inherited from the classical world was one based on community or public opinion, according to Paul Strohm in his history of conscience. Christianity brought an understanding of conscience that was inner, individual, and personal. Yet, this newer understanding carried with it the older one rooted in "public expectation," Strohm explains. Thus, from the start, "Christian conscience would always potentially serve two masters: its possessor or subject, on the one hand, and the doctrinal or theological views of its ecclesiastical sponsor, on the other."[26]

This tension helps explain how consciences can be dulled, conflicted, and even deformed. Our consciences are pulled at from within and without, from the Word, the Holy Spirit, and the world. Thus, the need for continual awakenings, sometimes great ones.

The reckoning we are facing as Evangelicals (and as Christians more generally) over rampant sexual abuse, abuse of power, racism, misogyny, and institutional corruption is evidence that we have been asleep, our eyes have been shut, and our consciences dulled or even seared. I doubt there are Christian leaders or institutions selling the healing powers of literal sheep bones these days. But if we understand the metaphor, we will see not only the bag of goods

---

25. FitzGerald, *Evangelicals*, 14.
26. Strohm, *Conscience*, 6–8.

that is being sold, but we might also see that those perpetrating the frauds are often hiding in plain sight.

If this is the case, then the real reform is not needed in them, it is needed in us—by which I mean mainly in me.

Bibliography

Augustine. *Confessions*. Translated by Sarah Ruden. New York: Modern Library, 2018.
Bebbington, David W. *Evangelicalism in Modern Britain: A History from the 1730s to the 1980s*. London: Taylor & Francis, 2003.
Chaucer, Geoffrey. *The Canterbury Tales*. In *The Riverside Chaucer*, edited by Larry D. Benson, 3–328. Boston: Houghton Mifflin, 1987.
Diamond, Jeremy. "Trump: I Could Shoot Somebody and I Wouldn't Lose Voters.'" *CNN*, January 24, 2016. https://www.cnn.com/2016/01/23/politics/donald-trump-shoot-somebody-support/index.html.
Du Mez, Kristin Kobes. "There Are No Real Evangelicals, Only Imaginary Ones." *Religion News Service*, February 6, 2019. https://religionnews.com/2019/02/06/there-are-no-real-evangelicals-only-imagined-ones.
FitzGerald, Frances. *The Evangelicals: The Struggle to Shape America*. New York: Simon and Schuster, 2017.
Guite, Malcolm. "Evolving Consciousness: Spiritual Experience in a Secular Age." Panel discussion, Scientific and Medical Network with the Fetzer Institute, London, November 30, 2019. https://youtu.be/zRFNM6mqLg4.
King, Martin Luther, Jr. *Where Do We Go from Here: Chaos or Community?* Boston: Beacon, 1968.
Luther, Martin. "To the Christian Nobility of the German Nation, Concerning the Reform of the Christian Estate 1520." In Vol. 44 of *Luther's Works: The Christian in Society 1*, edited by James Atkinson and Helmut Lehmann. Translated by Charles M. Jacobs. Philadelphia: Fortress, 1966.
McLuhan, Marshall. "Electric Consciousness and the Church." In *The Medium and the Light: Reflections on Religion and Media*, edited by Eric McLuhan and Jacek Szklarek, 79–88. Eugene, OR: Wipf & Stock, 2010.
NASB Lexicon. Bible Hub. https://biblehub.com/lexicon/john/14-6.htm.
R.E.M. "It's the End of the World as We Know It (and I Feel Fine)." *Document*, I.R.S. Records, 1987.
Shelley, Percy Bysshe. *A Defence of Poetry*. Edited by Mary Wollstonecraft Shelley. Indianapolis: Bobbs-Merrill, 1904.
Smith, Christian, and Melinda Lundquist Denton. *Soul Searching: The Religious and Spiritual Lives of American Teenagers*. New York: Oxford University Press, 2005.
Strohm, Paul. *Conscience: A Very Short Introduction*. Oxford: Oxford University Press, 2011.
Taylor, Charles. *Modern Social Imaginaries*. Durham: Duke University Press, 2004.
Trueman, Carl R. *The Rise and Triumph of the Modern Self: Cultural Amnesia, Expressive Individualism, and the Road to Sexual Revolution*. Wheaton, IL: Crossway, 2020.
Vernon, Mark. "The Mossy Face of Christ." *Mark Vernon—Talks and Thoughts*, podcast, June 14, 2022. https://www.buzzsprout.com/1574515/10791825-the-mossy-face-

of-christ-martin-shaw-talks-w-mark-vernon-about-an-unexpected-return-to-christianity.

———. *A Secret History of Christianity: Jesus, the Last Inkling, and the Evolution of Consciousness*. Winchester, UK: Christian Alternative, 2019.

Vernon, Mark, and Malcom Guite. "The Faith of the Inklings, with Malcolm Guite." Interview by Justin Brierley. *Unbelievable*, podcast, August 9, 2019. https://www.markvernon.com/the-faith-of-the-inklings-with-malcolm-guite.

Wright, N. T. "Paul and Caesar: A New Reading of Romans." In *A Royal Priesthood? The Use of the Bible Ethically and Politically: A Dialogue with Oliver O'Donovan*, edited by Craig Bartholomew et al., 173–93. Scripture and Hermeneutics Series 3. Grand Rapids: Zondervan Academic, 2002.

Wu, Kaidi, and David Dunning. "Unknown Unknowns: The Problem of Hypocognition." *Scientific American*, August 9, 2018. https://blogs.scientificamerican.com/observations/unknown-unknowns-the-problem-of-hypocognition/.

2

A Call for Prophetic Leadership

The Church's Recipe for Responding to White Christian Nationalism and the Great Replacement Theory

JONATHAN C. AUGUSTINE

> Christian nationalism is not unique because it is used to draw boundaries (of the symbolic or physical variety) around group membership. Many cultural frameworks or other social markers, religious or otherwise, are used by groups to draw boundaries between "us" and "them." But Christian nationalism is distinct from religiosity in a general sense. The two phenomena share a common tendency to imbue boundaries of group membership with ultimate, cosmic significance, to equate in-group members with divine election and righteousness and see out of group members as hell-bound instruments of the Devil himself.
> —ANDREW L. WHITEHEAD & SAMUEL L. PERRY,
> *TAKING AMERICA BACK FOR GOD*[1]

---

1. Whitehead and Perry, *Taking America Back for God*, 114.

Introduction

As a proud New Orleans native, I have no reservation in sharing that gumbo is my favorite food. I love the shrimp. I love the sausage. I love the chicken. I also love the okra. Gumbo brings diverse ingredients together, each maintaining their individuality, while simultaneously creating a collective community. As someone who also loves to cook gumbo, I know each diverse ingredient is supposed to complement the others, not compete against them. Shrimp complements sausage, just as chicken complements okra. Recent events have confirmed my theological belief that what's good in a gumbo should also be good in America.

A gumbo *is not* soup. It is also not the proverbial "melting pot" America was often described as in yesteryear. A gumbo's ingredients are not a blend or amalgamation where diverse ingredients, or perspectives, become one. With a theology of gumbo for a very divided America, I believe differences should be celebrated, instead of assimilated. Although I believe racial and ethnic diversity is good for America, as a contrast to my love of a gumbo's diversity, I wonder why some are so committed to white Christian nationalism and the great replacement theory that attempts to make America a bland soup.

Given America's factions, this chapter is about the church's recipe for a gumbo, my translation of the biblical term "reconciliation." Stated otherwise, this chapter is about the church's call to prophetic leadership in charting a path for progress, instead of maintaining a space where more factions become rooted in social intolerance.

America's Replacement Theory

On May 14, 2022, America witnessed another incident of racially motivated violence, one that went directly to my core, as a Black pastor, serving in the African Methodist Episcopal Church.

An eighteen-year-old white supremacist targeted a predominately Black community in Buffalo, New York, and plotted to kill Blacks shopping in a Tops grocery store. He drove more than two hundred miles, surveyed his target area, and opened fire, killing ten innocent people. He published a white manifesto that articulated a "replacement theory," espousing a fear that Blacks, Jews, and immigrants are replacing whites in America's hierarchy. The shooter's logic particularly hit me, because it was the same logic that motivated another white supremacist to write another white manifesto, and deliberately seek out and kill the Reverend Clementa C. Pinckney, a fellow AME pastor, and eight members of his Bible study at Mother Emmanuel AME Church, in Charleston, South Carolina, on June 17, 2015.

I once heard, "If violence is the language of the unheard, absolutism is the language of the insecure." The replacement theory fueling both assassins' violent attacks does not see America as a gumbo with diverse peoples living in community. Instead, it sees different races and ethnicities in "competition," with an associated uncertainty apparently creating insecurity. With soup, you have the security of knowing that each spoon provides the same thing. In eating a gumbo, however, you are sure to get something different. The absolutism of white supremacy and its replacement theory seeks an America where all "Others" are blended into a puree, instead of a diverse community.

White Christian Nationalism and Make America Great Again

The insecurity of Christian nationalists works to maintain the status quo by taking America through a period of regress, where complete citizen inclusion is being combatted by the dominant power structure. This dynamic manifests in the form of Christian nationalism or specifically, *white* Christian nationalism.

As Whitehead and Perry note in *Taking America Back for God*, Christian nationalism is a cultural and political framework that has little to do with any church orthodoxy, but everything to do with preservation of America's social order that has historically placed an increased value on white Protestantism, and a decreased value on "Others."[2] Christian nationalism embraces an "us against them" political framework where America is God's chosen nation—just like the Bible portrays the Israelites as God's chosen people—and any opposition to America's *original* operational structure is against God's will. Considering America's population changes, however, one must also consider the part contemporary demographics play in fueling *white* Christian nationalism.

In *The Flag and the Cross: White Christian Nationalism and the Threat to American Democracy*, Gorski and Perry argue,

> as white Christians approach minority status, white Christian nationalists are starting to turn against American democracy. After all, the basic principle of democratic government is majority rule. So long as white Christians were in the majority, they could call the shots. . . . Now faced with the prospect of minority

---

2. Whitehead and Perry, *Taking America Back for God*, ix–xi.

status themselves, some members of the old white majority are embracing authoritarian politics as a means of protecting their "freedom."[3]

White Christian nationalism's embrace of authoritarianism was seen in the January 6, 2021, insurrection; it was an attempt to protect their dominant cultural freedom.

In 2016, Donald Trump was elected president by speaking a language that emboldened the insecure demographic of replacement theorists. He promised to "Make America Great Again" by taking America back to its darkest days, where the bland soup of white Protestantism ruled the day. Although issues of race, ethnicity, and religion—especially related to Blacks, immigrants from Mexico, and Muslims entering the United States—were not new to presidential politics, Trump discussed them in more polarizing terms than ever before.[4] With a "whitelash" that responded to Barack Obama's presidency by embracing the Make America Great Again narrative and electing Trump in 2016, how could any "fair election" in 2020 result in Trump's defeat?

As violent vigilantes stormed the Capitol on January 6, 2021, many had paraphernalia indicating, "Stop the Steal: In God We Trust" and "Jesus Is My Savior, Trump Is My President." Some even carried life-size replicas of Jesus's cross. Peaceful protest is one thing. It is a right deeply ingrained in America's social fabric through the First Amendment. That right, however, stands in sharp contrast to the attack against democracy that occurred at the Capitol. Indeed, Mike Pence, Trump's vice president and a devout evangelical Christian who was presiding officer over the election certification, writes in *So Help Me God*, "I was angry at what I saw, how it desecrated the seat of our democracy and dishonored the patriotism of millions of our supporters who would never do such a thing here or anywhere else. To see fellow Americans ransacking the Capitol left me with a simmering indignation and the thought: Not here, not this . . . *not in America*."[5] To echo Gorski and Perry, America is supposed to be a democracy, not an authoritarian government. But white Christian nationalists did not want democracy. They wanted control.

The American Church's Recipe for Gumbo

Following the church's theological logic, an American gumbo recipe calls for social reconciliation and prophetic leadership. In the process of unpacking

---

3. Gorski and Perry, *Flag and the Cross*, 8 (internal citations omitted).
4. Sides, Tesler, and Vavreck, *Identity Crisis*, 80–81.
5. Pence, *So Help Me God*, 464 (emphasis original).

these two ingredients, I will also critique certain aspects of white Christian nationalism. After exploring Paul's theology of equality—what I call social reconciliation—I will highlight the need for prophetic leadership, as part of the *munus triplex* doctrine/threefold office and call on the American church to lead in the prophetic domain by following Jesus's example of "speaking truth to power," to demand equal treatment of all.

Gumbo is more than just my favorite food; it is also a recipe for life. If the American church can be an exemplar in this type of reconciliation, the church can also be a model for addressing the discord in society-at-large. When do we stop buying in to wedge issues? The American church must lead in "cooking community." This chapter is an invitation to join me in the kitchen!

Paul's Theology of Reconciliation: A Key Ingredient in the American Church's Gumbo Recipe

All this is from God, who reconciled us to himself through Christ, and has given us the ministry of reconciliation; that is, in Christ God was reconciling the world to himself, not counting their trespasses against them, and entrusting the message of reconciliation to us.
—2 Cor 5:18–19 NRSV

In *Called to Reconciliation: How the Church Can Model Justice, Diversity and Inclusion*, I note that the word reconciliation appears primarily in the Pauline corpus,[6] and argue that Paul's theology gives us: (1) salvific reconciliation, where humans are reconciled in their relationship to God, *through* Jesus; (2) social reconciliation, where humans are reconciled to one another, as equals, *because* of Jesus; and (3) civil reconciliation, an ethic of prophetic resistance that civically seeks out the principles of equality that are embedded in Scripture.[7] If "all" really means "all" and, "We hold these truths to be self-evident that all [people] are created equal," civil reconciliation and prophetic leadership demand that the American church speak out when America fails to live up to its creed. Popular examples of prophetic leaders, in their respective contexts, include Martin Luther King, Jr. and William J. Barber, II, in America, and Dietrich Bonhoeffer in Third Reich Germany.

Because the American church's gumbo recipe has little to do with theologies of the eschaton and salvation in the "kingdom-to-come," but is focused on equitable social relations in the "kingdom-at-hand," salvific reconciliation

---

6. Augustine, *Called to Reconciliation*, 18.
7. Augustine, *Called to Reconciliation*, 19–27.

is not further discussed herein, except to say that it is the foundation for social reconciliation and the prophetic witness of civil reconciliation, too. Paul writes, "For if while we were enemies, we were reconciled to God through the death of his Son, much more surely, having been reconciled, will we be saved by his life. But more than that, we even boast in God through our Lord Jesus Christ, through whom we have now received reconciliation" (Rom 5:10–11 NRSV).

Salvific reconciliation leads to social reconciliation because we are called to be reconcilers in a ministry Jesus left to the church (2 Cor 5:19). If there is no social ethic attached to reconciliation, it becomes part of an individualistic Christianity that can dangerously create a superficial discipleship by separating salvation from social transformation.[8] Although the church's gumbo recipe does not call for further discussions of salvation, it does call for heaping portions of social and civil reconciliation.

Social Reconciliation in Galatians

To conceptualize how we are reconciled to one another *because* of Jesus, consider Galatians. Paul's central focus is freedom, "not the freedom to consume or dominate, but the freedom to love and to be transformed even more in God's image and likeness."[9] Stated otherwise, social reconciliation requires the responsible use of a freedom to love and accept others as equal. In this regard, Galatians might be considered a letter to address ethnic differences within Christian communities.[10]

As Paul's missionary work proved successful and more Gentiles joined the church, the inevitable issue arose as to what relationship Gentile Christians should have toward Judaism with respect to Torah—the law of Moses. Paul wrote Galatians partially to insist that Gentile converts did not need to first convert to Judaism and become circumcised to become true Christians. His rebuke of several other itinerant preachers' theologies (as manifested through the epistle's polemics) firmly supports his argument that the Christ event brought equality to *all* people, Jew and Gentile alike.

In rejecting claims for Gentile circumcision (Gal 2:21—3:9), Paul shows a connection between salvific and social reconciliation, by emphasizing the unconditional nature of salvation *through* Jesus and how human beings are all equal, *because* of Jesus. Paul also shares what is arguably the New Testament's

---

8. Katongole and Rice, *Reconciling All Things*, 28.
9. Bedford, *Galatians*, 11.
10. Braxton, *No Longer Slaves*, 93.

most egalitarian passage of Scripture, "for in Christ Jesus you all are children of God through faith. As many of you as were baptized into Christ have clothed yourselves with Christ. There is no longer Jew or Greek, there is no longer slave or free, there is no longer male and female, for all of you are one in Christ Jesus" (Gal 3:26–28 NRSV). While Paul's reference was likely from a baptismal liturgy,[11] this same theology of equality is apparent in several of Paul's other writings, too (see, e.g., Rom 10:12; 1 Cor 12:13; and Col 3:11). Moreover, Paul's most definitive statement on complete equality within the church addresses the hotbed issues of social division: ethnic relationships (Jew nor Greek), social class (slave nor free), and gender relationships (male and female).[12]

Returning to my assertion that the authenticity of a gumbo is different from the amalgamation of a melting pot, I once gave a lecture discussing Galatians, and an attendee asked about Paul's language, "for all of you *are one* in Christ Jesus" (Gal 3:28 NRSV, emphasis added). For her, this suggests the melting pot of yesteryear, instead of the gumbo I argue for today. I believe Paul's theology of oneness is not about eliminating differences. It is about eliminating dominance. Gumbo celebrates differences, while also eliminating dominance. Indeed, all should be welcome in Jesus's church, regardless of race, ethnicity, gender, or economic status. This obliteration of dominance, through baptism into the body of Christ, was particularly revolutionary for Paul, considering the patriarchal and social class structures of the Greco-Roman world in which he lived.

I argue that social reconciliation is comprised of three requisite actions: (1) equal treatment of others; (2) forgiveness for previous transgressions; and (3) recognizing that forgiveness is a part of the ministry of reconciliation Jesus left to the church.[13] These required actions are predicated on the understanding that America's historic imbalance of power, embedded in class structures, continues to exist today, just as it existed in Paul's Greco-Roman world. The three actions, therefore, presuppose that one class has been dominant, and the other subservient, according to each category. With respect to the social construct of race, for example, white has been the dominant class and Black has been subservient. Similarly, with respect to gender, male has been dominant, and female has been subservient. These social imbalances have always existed in America.

---

11. Augustine, *Called to Reconciliation*, 42.
12. Braxton, *No Longer Slaves*, 93.
13. Augustine, *Called to Reconciliation*, 49–52.

1. Equal Treatment of Others

White Christian nationalism is the antithesis of equal treatment of Others. In framing it, "Otherism" deals with racial minorities, immigrants, and Jews, ranking them as subordinate to white Anglo-Saxon Protestants and their dominant cultural norms. Otherism manifests in voter suppression laws that seek to create obstacles for minorities and wage-earning workers to fully participate in America's electoral process. This has been apparent in the politics of redistricting both state legislative and congressional districts, as well as the reduction of polling places in minority neighborhoods, in the wake of the Supreme Court's infamous ruling in *Shelby County v. Holder* (2013), a decision that has all but eviscerated the protections afforded minorities under the Voting Rights Act of 1965. Regrettably, my adopted home state of North Carolina often leads in attempts to undermine democracy.[14]

Further, the "Make America Great Again" narrative cannot be limited to a political slogan associated with Trump's 2016 campaign victory or 2020 election defeat. It represents a regressive mindset that is rooted in a white Christian nationalism that motivates antisemitism against Jews, and racial intolerance against immigrants—not to mention the violence perpetuated against Asian Americans, as Trump often pejoratively referenced COVID-19 as the "China Virus" or the "Kung Flu." By following Paul's example of equal treatment of others (Gal 3:26–28), the American church has an opportunity to show society at large how a good gumbo might taste.

2. Forgiveness for Previous Transgressions

Social reconciliation also requires humans to forgive one another, just as God forgives humans. In *Embodying Forgiveness*, L. Gregory Jones addresses the imbalance of power dynamics that is inherent in class structures. He writes, "The practice of reconciling forgiveness calls us to unlearn the language that confuses, dominates, and controls and learn the 'redemptive language' that enables us to sustain community. Issues of forgiveness and reconciliation invariably involve issues of power."[15] Forgiveness for previous transgressions—one of the reciprocal obligations associated with power imbalances—is not for the faint of heart.

In *No Future Without Forgiveness*, Archbishop Desmond Tutu, the Anglican cleric and the first head of the South African Truth and Reconciliation Commission, describes Nelson Mandela's magnanimity, after becoming the

---

14. Leloudis and Korstad, *Fragile Democracy*.
15. Jones, *Embodying Forgiveness*, 190.

first post-apartheid democratically elected South African head of state, for *forgiving* and inviting his (white) former jailer to an honored seat at his presidential inauguration. Mandela did so, not in jest, but in complete sincerity, as the embodiment of forgiveness and reconciliation.[16] My point is that members of a subservient class must be willing to do the hard work of forgiveness, as it relates to the dominant class. But there is also a reciprocal obligation. Members of the dominant class must do the hard work of changing their behaviors and perhaps abandoning class structures that have systemically inured to their benefit. Indeed, these reciprocal obligations involve the complementary dynamics of repenting and forgiving, where the dominant classes deal with having done the wrong, and the subservient classes forgive, after having suffered the wrong.[17]

3. Recognizing that Forgiveness Is a Part of the Ministry of Reconciliation Jesus Left to the Church

I believe the greatest example of forgiveness was Jesus's exclamation during his brutal crucifixion: "Father forgive them; for they do not know what they are doing" (Luke 23:34 NRSV). In emphasizing the importance of forgiveness as a part of the ministry of reconciliation Jesus left to the church, Paul's theology is again appropriate. He writes, "So if anyone is in Christ, there is a new creation: everything old has passed away; see, everything has become new! All this is from God, who reconciled us to himself through Christ, and has given us the ministry of reconciliation . . . entrusting the message of reconciliation to us" (2 Cor 5:17–19 NRSV). Stated otherwise, if we take Scripture seriously, the church must acknowledge that we are not only forgiven by God but also entrusted with the message of God's forgiveness for the world.[18]

In building on social reconciliation, as a theological outgrowth of salvific reconciliation, and showing it as an essential ingredient in the American church's recipe for gumbo, I now discuss civil reconciliation, an aspect of prophetic leadership that often manifests through preaching to mobilize congregations.

---

16. Tutu, *No Future Without Forgiveness*, 10.
17. Liechty, "Putting Forgiveness in Its Place," 60.
18. Jones, *Embodying Forgiveness*, 38.

The Munus Triplex Doctrine and Model of Prophetic Leadership: A Call for More Modern Day Prophets to Preach "Politics"

> But how are they to call on one in whom they have not believed? And how are they to believe in one of whom they have never heard? And how are they to hear without someone to proclaim him?
>
> —Romans 10:14 NRSV

America's polarization from white Christian nationalists and replacement theorists is evidenced by attitudes related to things like voting rights, the need for meaningful immigration reform, and widespread acts of antisemitism. Although I believe the church is uniquely called on to address social polarization through prophetic leadership, I also recognize that many pastors do not want to be "political." Some pastors feel politics has no place in the church. To paraphrase Martin Luther King Jr., they only discuss salvation in the kingdom-to-come and omit addressing social injustices in the kingdom-at-hand. I believe pastors who do not address political issues from the pulpit are preaching a truncated gospel.

In addressing the nature of Christianity's *political* birth amid Jewish marginalization within the Roman empire, King writes in his first book, *Stride Toward Freedom: The Montgomery Story*, "The Christian ought to always be challenged by any protest against unfair treatment of the poor, for Christianity is itself such a protest."[19] In considering Israel's history, before Jesus came as a *spiritual* liberator, the exodus from Egypt was a *political* liberation. It drew a line of demarcation where the biblical narrative moved from individualistic to communal, making the exodus a political event, as an entire class of subjugated people moved toward liberty.[20] Accordingly, Moses was "political" and the ethic of his prophetic leadership required him to tell Pharoah that God says, "Let my people go!" (Exod 5:1; 9:1 NRSV).

The word *politics*, as translated from Greek, simply means "affairs of the cities."[21] Consequently, when the American church gets "political," it is not wearing the "Team Red" or "Team Blue" colors of partisanship. Instead, its political activism occurs when faith compels a social (re)action. Let's consider a few biblical examples. Amos's cries for justice in the northern kingdom of Israel are most certainly political (Amos 5:4, 24). When the famed Hebrew boys, Shadrach, Meshach, and Abednego, engage in civil disobedience by

---

19. King, *Stride Toward Freedom*, 93.
20. Hendricks, *Politics of Jesus*, 14.
21. Hardin, "Preaching Politics," 3.

refusing to obey King Nebuchadnezzar's dictates, they too are political (Dan 3). As John writes from the penal colony of Patmos to the seven churches being oppressed by an unjust Roman government, he is extremely political (Rev 1:9). Moreover, all these examples of "politics" are lauded in Christianity.

In *When Prophets Preach: Leadership and the Politics of the Pulpit*, I call for pastors to address issues like mass incarceration, the separation of migrant children from their families at the US/Mexico border, and environmental degradation by engaging in prophetic preaching. "Prophetic preaching is not just about biblical texts, as in preaching from the Bible's Prophetic Books. It is instead about promulgating God's word from a liberative perspective that focuses on justice and equality within both the church and society at large and promotes human empowerment in response to social marginalization."[22] I believe prophetic preaching was the hallmark and inauguration of Jesus's public ministry, as he began by proclaiming, "The Spirit of the Lord is upon me, because he has anointed me to bring good news to the poor. He has sent me to proclaim release to the captives and recovery of sight to the blind, to let the oppressed go free, to proclaim the year of the Lord's favor" (Luke 4:18–19 NRSV).

In what we might call Jesus's first sermon, he announced that the reason for his anointing and purpose for his worldly mission are one and the same: to proclaim radical economic, political, and social change.[23] Jesus's ministry was prophetic because he addressed social marginalization resulting from class structures. Moreover, the combined reasons for Jesus's ministry, to address salvation in the kingdom-to-come and social injustices in the kingdom-at-hand, made him political too.

In his time-honed expression, Karl Barth said, "The preacher should preach with the Bible in one hand and the newspaper in the other."[24] In addition to giving context to Scripture and making God's word relevant to the contemporary church, Barth's implication is also that preachers should not be afraid to address newsworthy issues, or *political* issues. The willingness to lead in such a way is part of the threefold office, also known as the *munus triplex* doctrine, that explores Jesus's leadership as a prophet, priest, and king (royal). It is through the lens of prophetic leadership that the prophetic preaching and the ministry of reconciliation come together.

---

22. Augustine, *When Prophets Preach*, 4.
23. Hendricks, *Politics of Jesus*, 7–8.
24. Augustine, *When Prophets Preach*, 6.

The Threefold Office

Although the terminology of threefold office is ecclesial, a corollary highlight of secular leadership terms may help provide context in my call for more leaders to preach prophetically in the American church. "Direct leadership takes charge, like a king. Relational leadership offers care and enhances others' self-worth, much like a priest. And instrumental leadership motivates others into new ways of seeing and acting, like a prophet."[25] Inasmuch as Jesus's leadership was perfect in all three domains, humans will naturally gravitate to one type of leadership more than the others. While direct and relational leadership are both important in serving the body of Christ, the American church's gumbo recipe requires more pastors to exercise *instrumental* leadership and speak out from a moral imperative rooted in the prophetic domain.

Kingly (royal) leadership is direct. It charters a course of action and builds optimism during the inevitability of crisis. It can also convince people to move in unforeseen ways. With Jesus as an exemplar in calling Peter and Andrew as his first disciples, "Follow me, and I will make you fish for people" (Matt 4:19 NRSV), Jesus exhibited royal leadership. Similarly, pastors who successfully led congregations during the COVID-19 shutdown and who helped transition them into virtual operation, while pivoting church meetings from in-person gatherings to the "new norm" of Zoom, led in the royal domain, too.

Priestly leaders help create meaning through story, by offering conciliatory leadership and consensus building, especially in times of despair. To again consider Jesus as the exemplar, he spoke to the disciples prior to his anticipated crucifixion to build consensus and offer solace. "Do not let your hearts be troubled. Believe in God, believe also in me" (John 14:1 NRSV). The most popular example of priestly leadership in the modern context is a pastor visiting the sick and leading the inevitable celebration of life.

Finally, prophetic leadership requires the church to expose systems that are unjust and unfair, while "speaking truth to power" (institutions of power) in attempting to change those systems.[26] Indeed, Jesus is the ultimate prophetic leadership exemplar. Consider again Jesus's initial sermon. In the contemporary context, we might say he was addressing social justice issues like poverty, food insecurity, and mass incarceration (Luke 4:18–19). Those issues clearly go well beyond individualistic piety and salvation in the kingdom-to-come. They go to the heart of systems that often marginalize communities and perpetuate social inequities in the kingdom-at-hand. With a foundation now laid for prophetic leadership, I move to the importance of prophetic preaching.

---

25. Augustine, *When Prophets Preach*, 9.
26. Augustine, *When Prophets Preach*, 10.

PART ONE: CHALLENGES

The American Prophet Must Preach

The call for prophetic preaching seeks to engage more in the American church as twenty-first century prophets. Someone must preach that Christian nationalism and xenophobia are wrong, especially when Christians vilify Others. Because of the structure of so many churches, "getting political" will almost always begin with preaching. Indeed, the task of *prophetic* preaching is to move the congregation's perspective from more individual concerns to broader social issues, as they consider their place in the larger world. In *Leading with the Sermon*, Willimon reminds us that it is through preaching that God's people are led, or violently jolted, toward new descriptions of reality.[27] Remember, the task of instrumental leaders is to move people to see things in ways not before seen. This is the work of prophetic preaching.

Conclusion

Who will preach a reconciling gospel of equity and inclusion, moving congregants to see new possibilities in a gumbo that were not before seen in a melting pot? Within the framework of the threefold office, prophetic leadership is responsive to social circumstances. America's current circumstances of polarization and division are a clarion call for contemporary prophets to preach, in the image of Jesus, a *prophetic* leader who was also political.

Congregations are moved by preaching! The confluence of white Christian nationalism and the great replacement theory is more than enough reason for churches to get political, if they are led by prophetic preachers. Personal piety and social justice are not mutually exclusive. Instead, they are necessary ingredients in the American church's recipe for gumbo, along with a theology of equality that is rooted in reconciliation. I hope this chapter's readers will join me in the kitchen. Moreover, with an ode to Barth, I hope you will also join me in the pulpit, with your Bible and a newspaper.

Bibliography

Augustine, Jonathan C. *Called to Reconciliation: How the Church Can Model Justice, Diversity and Inclusion*. Grand Rapids: Baker Academic, 2022.
———. *When Prophets Preach: Leadership and the Politics of the Pulpit*. Minneapolis: Fortress, 2023.
Bedford, Nancy Elizabeth. *Galatians*. Louisville: Westminster John Knox, 2016.
Braxton, Brad. *No Longer Slaves: Galatians and African American Experience*. Collegeville, MN: Liturgical, 2002.

27. Willimon, *Leading with the Sermon*, 10.

Gorski, Philip S., and Samuel L. Perry. *The Flag and the Cross: White Christian Nationalism and the Threat to American Democracy.* New York: Oxford University Press, 2022.

Hardin, Crystal J. "Preaching Politics: Not Yes or No, but How." In *Prophetic Preaching: The Hope or Curse of the Church?*, edited by Ian S. Markham and Crystal J. Hardin, 1–14. New York: Church, 2020.

Hendricks, Obery M., Jr. *The Politics of Jesus: Rediscovering the True Revolutionary Nature of Jesus' Teachings and How They Have Been Corrupted.* New York: Three Leaves, 2006.

Jones, L. Gregory. *Embodying Forgiveness: A Theological Analysis.* Grand Rapids: Eerdmans, 1995.

Katongole, Emmanuel, and Chris Rice. *Reconciling All Things: A Christian Vision for Justice, Peace and Healing.* Downers Grove, IL: IVP, 2008.

King, Martin Luther, Jr. *Stride Toward Freedom: The Montgomery Story.* Repr., Eugene, OR: Wipf & Stock, 2001.

Leloudis, James L., and Robert R. Korstad. *Fragile Democracy: The Struggle Over Race and Voting Rights in North Carolina.* Chapel Hill: University of North Carolina Press, 2020.

Liechty, Joseph. "Putting Forgiveness in Its Place: The Dynamics of Reconciliation." In *Explorations in Reconciliation: New Directions in Theology*, edited by David Tombs and Joseph Liechty, 59–68. Burlington, VT: Ashgate, 2006.

Pence, Mike. *So Help Me God.* New York: Simon & Schuster, 2022.

Sides, John, Michael Tesler, and Lynn Vavreck. *Identity Crisis: The 2026 Presidential Campaign and the Battle for the Meaning of America.* Princeton: Princeton University Press, 2018.

Tutu, Desmond. *No Future Without Forgiveness.* New York: Doubleday, 1999.

Whitehead, Andrew L., and Samuel L. Perry. *Taking America Back for God: Christian Nationalism in the United States.* New York: Oxford University Press, 2020.

Willimon, William H. *Leading with the Sermon: Preaching as Leadership.* Minneapolis: Fortress, 2020.

3

In Search of Disciples of Christ

ELIZABETH CONDE-FRAZIER

INTRODUCTION

JESUS IS THE TRUTH. An encounter with the one who is truth is transforming. Transformation is the eventual goal of reconstruction for the evangelical church. Reconstruction is not transformation, but a step toward it.

Paul speaks about edifying the body. The Greek term he uses is *katartismon*, which is a medical term for fixing a broken bone that was set wrong and therefore must be broken anew and reset. If the bone is not broken and reset, mobility is lost and, at worst, the bone becomes infected and can cause death. When you break a bone everything around it such as ligaments and tendons seek to protect it by contracting. When you reset it, you need to stretch everything that was contracted. The process entails pain that leads to healing and wholeness, which in the Hebrew Scriptures are words that mean salvation. If our desire is to reconstruct with the purpose of edifying the body of Christ, reconstruction is the working out of our salvation.

Evangelicals come from a diversity of social locations, which affects how we understand reconstruction. During the Center for Pastor Theologians' annual conference of which this paper was a part, one African American sister suggested that instead of considering things through the lens of fairness, we should rather consider them through the lens of grace. The response to her suggested that this was an issue of semantics. Let me assure you that from the social location of someone who has had ancestors who were enslaved, to offer grace instead of fairness is not about semantics. Rather it is an amazing gift. To look at how evangelical theology rationalized slavery through the lens of fairness will make it weigh much heavier upon you. Grace, however, offers an easier way to pave the path toward reconstruction.

Social location also means that what is at stake in this process is different for some of us. My husband is African American; I come from migrant parents; my grandmother was Taína. Racism and colonization have meant and continue to mean death to us and to my children in this country, while for others, it can be a matter of intellectual or simple theological considerations.

Power and Humility

Reconstruction begins as a work of the Holy Spirit. It is only the Holy Spirit who can lead us into reconstruction. Therefore, we submit to the Holy Spirit throughout this dialogue. This means that we take on an attitude of humility. Humility is at the center of our moral lives. It is not a low self-regard but instead, it is thinking of ourselves with sober judgement (see Rom 12:3). This allows us to see ourselves in relation to others, knowing who we are and who we are not so that we do not usurp the place of another. This changes the relationships of power between us. Colonialism, which organized the world according to race, created an order where not everyone was considered human to the same degree. This allowed for the colonizers to usurp the self-determination of peoples, and therefore to take over their lands and to force persons into exploitative servitude-enslavement based on these relational understandings. This is *power over* and subjugation.

There are three types of power: *power over*, *power from within*, and *power with*.[1] *Power over* is the type of power we most often find in our society and is based on domination and authority. One person or group can determine the behavior of another person or group. *Power over* affects the spheres of relationship. It affects our bodies, minds, and spirits. *Power over* is power that bankrupts. This is the type of power that we wish to see transformed.

Power from within is power that arises from the building of connections and bonding with other people and the environment. It is power that awakens a person's abilities and potential. *Power from within* is what we strive for in our teaching and ministries. It is the type of power that we affirm through worship and sharing our lives for the benefit of one another. It is relational.

---

1. In the following, I use language and definitions adapted from Wink, *Naming the Powers*.

The power of Jesus is present in weakness in order to banish powerlessness. He brings out the powers of the weak, which are shared powers. So *power with* is the type of power shared among persons who value each other as equals. *Power with* includes respectful caring, mutual influence and shared power. *Power with* is fragile and fluid and requires disciplined listening, patience, openness, and solidarity.

The social construction of racism is very far from the biblical understanding that we are all created in the image of God—an understanding that places all of us in covenantal relationship with our Creator and with one another. This is righteousness. We come to this dialogue whose goal is to begin a process of reconstruction with humility. We come in the spirit of the publican praying at the altar rather than the Pharisee. We are all created in the image of God, we seek to bring out the power we each have for responding to Jesus as disciples, as people whose loyalties are first and foremost to Jesus as Lord because we seek to promote life—through the values of the *basileia*—the reign of Christ.[2]

Please allow me to call our attention to two well-known biblical characters—Noah and Abraham. Noah was a man recognized for his obedience. He had followed all of God's commands with regards to the building of the ark and the gathering of the animals. In all this journey Noah's voice is silent. He simply obeys. But as the narrative unfolds, Noah is found by his sons in a drunken stupor. What happened? Jewish midrash offers the argument that perhaps Noah was not able to face the challenges of beginning all over again. Perhaps he was dealing with survivor guilt. These things will paralyze us. Noah did not have courage but fear. In turn, he is compared with Abraham, another character recognized for his obedience to the point of being willing to sacrifice his son to God. When faced with a similar situation where God is about to destroy the city where his nephew Lot is living, Abraham dares to have a dialogue with God where he asks God to consider the decision about destruction in light of the possibility that there might be a few righteous persons amid the inhabitants. This is beyond obedience, for it is responsibility for the welfare of fellow humanity. This responsibility balances blind obedience such as that evoked by Nazis where Christians found themselves implicated in the horrors of that regime. This responsibility demonstrates love not fear. Hey, Abraham did not live in the city, why should he care? Oh, his nephew's family lived there. He felt a connection; that connection stirred up compassion in him and compassion courage. Not sympathy: "Oh my goodness did you see

---

2. I use the Greek term *basileia* instead of "kingdom" or "reign," which evoke in our imagination male-dominated and hierarchical orders. The Greek term is neutral, allowing a fuller sense of imagined new orders.

that? What a pity," but compassion: "This cannot go on, all this death. Jesus help us. Let's do something. Please, Lord, help us know your will here!"

History and Responsibility

This is an important detail for our consideration in the light of distorted relationships with one another. Connection helps us to feel love expressed by responsibility. Responsibility evokes in us feelings of identification with a sense of equality based on the fragility of our human nature. We live our lives in a historical context. It is within this historical context that the reality of the *basileia* must be made a reality. When we do not take responsibility for what has taken place in our historical context, we fall from right relationship with one another. Like Noah, we do not have the insight, the imagination, or the moral courage to reconstruct.

Racism has a history in this country, and Evangelicals who wish to reconstruct must take responsibility for our complicity in the heinous acts in the history of racism. As Evangelicals we have played a role, both in active and not so active ways, in the perpetuation of the evils of slavery and Jim Crow and, today, of police brutality and other forms of violence in the lives of persons of color as well as the more seemingly invisible, insidious forms that racism has taken on. This responsibility is a needed ethical expression of our obedience to God. I cannot say, "Oh I was not there. It happened a long time ago. Let's get over it." We are responsible even today to acknowledge that what preceded us has created the roots of what informs us today. We are harvesting the fruit of this history which continues to privilege some and take life away from others. God makes us responsible and calls us to account for our actions and silences.

This responsibility grieves us for the Spirit of God in us is grieved. If you feel grieved reading this, praise God, for the Spirit is still among us and has not been quenched. But know that this grieving is not meant to lead us into guilt. Guilt is like stagnant waters where parasites and disease lurk and grow. Grieving is meant to lead us to repentance—the place where we turn to the Holy Spirit's help in our past and present complicities to craft a forward future that looks like reconciliation and justice for all peoples and nations. We turn 180 degrees in a direction that points toward responsible obedience.

In *The Color of Compromise*, Jemar Tisby tells the history of the complicity of the American church in racism.[3] In it, chapter after chapter, he tells of how the social conscience of the church was formed by the immoral choices it made in the interest of their economic benefits. We see how even from the

---

3. Tisby, *Color of Compromise*.

earliest colonial era a convenient set of categories was formed to separate the physical from the spiritual so that the enslaved peoples could be saved spiritually but not physically from the oppression of slavery. You could baptize them but receiving the sacrament (grace) did not mean that they were to pass into freedom. Theology was being formed to maintain the economic interests intact. This was not the rock of Christ's truth but the sands of distortions of the image of God in each other: unrighteousness and injustice, the marring and muddying of grace.

To cover up the way to the unraveling of the lies of racism in all its forms, our theology obscured the way to salvation or liberation for the oppressed. Sin was defined as an individual reality, and the way to undo it was one by one through the trickle down of each individual Christian who accepted Jesus as personal savior. However, racism is a complex and intricate system constructed by social, political, philosophical, scientific, and religious dimensions. It created a social construction of lies that would cement the laws, the habits of the heart, and everyday living of slavery and other forms of racism across our history. It is a systemic and structural sin. But we have argued against such understandings of sin and salvation, even labelling them as communist, and therefore anathema, so as to place them far from ourselves, our consciousness, our set of beliefs and requirements of obedience or loyalty to Jesus. To construct a hope of dealing with racism through personal or individual efforts is to construct a failed praxis from the start. To present a hope to peoples of heaven as the only way out of their sufferings from oppression distorts heaven and the glory of God. It places an unbalanced and distorted vision and attention upon our eschatology while also distorting eschatology because we use it as a substitute for the work of undoing the structural sin of racism. All of this has been a work of "co-opting the faith to buttress white supremacy."[4]

The demand for raw materials and the products made from them grew into a systemic lasciviousness. Lasciviousness is a word that encapsulates what happens when desire for something blinds us from seeing what it costs another human being to satisfy that desire. Lasciviousness objectifies human beings created to be equal to us. Our economy then and now is fabricated out of greed and lasciviousness and runs on cheap labor, that of the different enslaved peoples: the new and varied immigrants, prisoners, and all those whose hopes for a better life are exploited with false promises so that they fall into the traps of human traffickers. This requires that we continue to promote the distorted images of those different from ourselves, those whom we have relegated to the margins for our use and personal benefit. We therefore promote theologies of conquest, we label the bodies of those we objectify, and we

4. Tisby, *Color of Compromise*, 22.

see their communities through the lens of deficit so that even our Christian charity is not love but a belittling of those communities.

We need to acknowledge that efforts toward reconciliation have taken place, and through them we have denounced racist actions of the past and have even written public documents of repentance asking for forgiveness of the groups we have wronged. But we have not constructed with our actions the types of movements or structures that would assure the strength and duration of the implications that we all hoped these efforts would have. Naively or neglectfully, we have acted as if these initial events or efforts were enough. Instead, when the trumpets of hateful and racist rhetoric were echoed by our previous president cloaked in "Make America Great Again" garb, these efforts were compromised. Tisby recounts how "Russell Moore, president of the Southern Baptist Convention's Ethics and Religious Liberty Commission, vocally opposed Trump during the primaries. . . . He called evangelical support of Trump 'illogical'" and suggested "that Evangelicals might risk losing support among black people by supporting Trump." Moore asked if in the midst of the work of racial reconciliation Evangelicals were "ready to trade unity with our black and brown brothers and sisters for this angry politician?"[5] The answer to his question came when his job was threatened by the white Evangelicals of his denomination. Tisby quotes the Pew Research Center statistics, which show how White Evangelical regular churchgoers were the most supportive of Trump to the tune of 75 to over 80 percent.[6] Such data exposes the inadequacy of the recent reconciliation efforts and the perseverance of the differences between us in spite of two decades of reconciliation work.[7] Do you wonder why we feel betrayed, and can you see how each betrayal breeds deeper and deeper distrust?

It makes us ask if the foundation of Christ was ever laid. In the parable of the two foundations, Jesus compares the differences between the sand and rock foundations to people "who hear my words and do them," versus those "who hear and do not do them." Those who hear and even call him "Lord, Lord" but do not obey or act in ways that demonstrate loyalty have built on sands of lies, not the rock of loyalty to Jesus as true Lord (Matt 7:21, 24–27).

---

5. Moore, "Have Evangelicals," quoted in Tisby, *Color of Compromise*, 188.
6. Smith, "Among White Evangelicals," quoted in Tisby, *Color of Compromise*, 189.
7. Tisby, *Color of Compromise*, 189.

PART ONE: CHALLENGES

HEARERS AND DOERS

Knowledge of the Scriptures that is only cognitively based runs the risk of becoming a modern-day Gnosticism. To truly know the Scriptures, which reveal an incarnational God, we need to engage them through other types of knowledge that allow for relational and incarnational understandings to take place. Scriptures cannot be fully understood until we are actually in the place of obedience—pursuing actions of alignment with the Scriptures. The journey of walking with the Spirit into such actions brings about a deeper understanding that thinking about those Scriptures alone cannot give to us. The Scriptures are a *dabar*—word. *Dabar* is the Hebrew notion that the word, once spoken, takes form, becomes a happening. Isaiah understands this when it says: "So is my word that goes out from my mouth: It will not return to me empty, but will accomplish what I desire and achieve the purpose for which I sent it" (Isa 55:11 NIV).

Has the word come back empty among us? How can this be when, as Evangelicals, recognition of the biblical authority for the purpose of our faith and commitment to it are our trademarks? I must ask in the light of this: Are we Christians? Have we instead pretended to be to ourselves and to others?

I am a Latina *evangélica*. This means that my roots in Evangelicalism come through the Latin American legacy, which today is characterized by the theology of *Misión Integral*. I humbly offer some insights from *Misión Integral* for reconstruction.[8] René Padilla describes a theological method for *Misión Integral* as the integration between Scripture and present obedience through a synthetic act in which the past of the Scripture and the present of our context, word, and Spirit, are brought together. This is a theology engaged in dialogue with both Scripture and the concrete situation; an approach concerned with the historical, the today and now, manifestation of the *basileia*. If the word cannot be clearly seen by those around us, then it has not taken form in us. It is like an ovum that fails to implant itself in the uterus of the mother and is miscarried. How many miscarried sermons have been preached from our pulpits?

The incarnation of the word of God not only holds to evangelical principles in the pursuit of a contextual method but demands that as disciples of Christ we stand in a prophetic tradition that desires a better world where justice and liberty reign. This is the integration of theology, ethics, and action that Orlando Costas writes about. It is evident when we make responsible decisions in respect to social, economic, political, biological, ecological, and cultural issues in order to build community, struggle for a just society, and

---

8. For a presentation and contextual analysis of the authors of *Misión Integral* in English see Heaney, *Contextual Theology for Latin America*.

enable people to live in freedom.⁹ Faith is not an intellectual question but must be made evident in our daily life commitments. It does not take much to discern injustice: Do you hear anyone saying that their lives are being destroyed? Do you see human life being deformed? Does everyone live in the comfort of safety that you do? Are there persons who are at risk as far as their health, their quality of education, their ability to walk around without having to ask how they might be perceived because of their skin color, their effervescent curls? Are there persons living without shade from the sun or without safe water or in a food desert? Then hello, we have a commitment to use all our spheres of influence to make a difference.

Samuel Escobar promotes "a courageous presence of advocates of compassion and justice because the church understands a new sense of history in which it sees herself as a history-making body of believers through whom God sends his gospel of salvation" at every dimension of life.[10]

Costas defines idolatry as "the choice to abandon partially or completely the order of things created by God, and to seek to live in a world of one's own construction."[11] From its inception, the construction of race was a social construct for the benefit of those who would rape and steal our land, our sovereignty and our livelihood, our dignity and freedom as human beings created in the image of God. We are a bunch of idolaters. This is not just an issue of our theology. We have distorted our theology to mask and accommodate our sins. This is an issue of life and death at all dimensions: spiritual, physical, emotional, economic, cultural, political, social, and moral. It is about here and now and the afterlife.

Winnowing is the traditional way of making the dried grains fall from a height using shovels and a sieve. The quality grains that are heavy fall vertically while the weightless chaff and straw get blown away by the wind. Thus, winnowing is effective only when there is wind. But fear not, a winnowing machine has been designed so that farmers no longer must depend on natural wind to begin the process of winnowing. The machine has a fan that can be rotated by pedaling and the velocity of the wind generated can be controlled by the speed of pedaling. I hope that the conference in which I presented this paper has and will be like a winnowing where the Spirit will blow and show us where the quality grains are. If we have not enough Spirit, then fear not, for those of us who have come to enter into this dialogue together will be like a winnowing machine. However, even those of us conducting the process of winnowing will be counted as chaff if we imitate the same spirit that has

9. See Escobar, "Vivir el Evangelio," 11–13; Costas, "La vida en el Espíritu," 105–12.
10. Escobar, *Liberation Themes*, 53.
11. Costas, "Pecado y salvación en América Latina," 271–87.

distorted our perceptions, relationships, daily living, habits of being, structures, knowledges, and actions. Racism requires two forces to stay up. Those who act into it and accommodate it and those who also accommodate it by learning to be receptacles. Even I, as a Latina, need to denounce it.

Now who bears the greater cost for denouncing racism in a society of *power over*? Who has the greater responsibility? How do we denounce racism? One way suggested by Tisby is by standing against viable symbols of racism promoted in public places. Tisby also speaks about reparations and how we can help fund the efforts of the African American community to minister in more creative ways because they have the funding to do so, as white churches share their resources—and I would add—with no strings attached.[12] Among other things, Tisby also speaks to expanding our white theological canon of orthodoxy by valuing Black theology and other forms of liturgy and Christian expressions such as Latine kinship theologies that come from our sufferings and resilience.[13] I would say that these bring a depth of faith that will be enriching to not just the Evangelicals but the church at large.

One suggestion he makes especially caught my attention. It may be true that all of us here are appalled by the actions and slogans of Evangelicals of the far right, slogans such as "Jesus, guns, and babies." We do not want to be identified as the same ilk of Evangelical. Tisby suggests conducting nonviolent direct-action protests toward other Christians and their institutions as a way of demanding change of our own.[14]

Pastor David Swanson contends that we need to become true disciples of Jesus by rethinking our liturgies and communal practices to reform ourselves and become capable of moving toward solidarity. One practice explains that worship calls us away from our daily activities, and then calls us to consciously identify by name that we are being called away from our daily practices of racism—calling out what these specific practices are in contextual and not abstract ways. This makes us more aware of them and hopefully makes us feel the conviction necessary to stay away from such practices. For those who feel they need to start in more familiar places to move toward discipleship and thus away from racism, Swanson's book is a fruitful read.[15] My friends, there is no dearth of books on these topics, only a sense of commitment beyond the reading.

---

12. Tisby, *Color of Compromise*, 200.
13. Tisby, *Color of Compromise*, 202
14. Tisby, *Color of Compromise*, 212.
15. See Swanson, *Rediscipling the White Church*.

The winnowing process is to reap the fruit, which is wheat. Wheat is used to make bread. Jesus is the bread of life. The church is called not to be successful but to bear fruit.

Conclusion

My colleague, Dr. Javier Viera, once preached a mighty and very simple sermon.[16] In it, he opened our eyes to some deep insights about the rich man and Lazarus. We are all familiar with the story. Remember the scene where the rich man finds himself in hell, and he sees Lazarus in the bosom of Abraham? He asks Abraham—not Lazarus—that Abraham might send Lazarus to give him a drop of water to cool his tongue. Viera brings our attention to the sense of privilege that still informs the rich man. He still thinks that things work the same way for him in hell. He thinks that he need only use his influence. He thinks that Lazarus is still supposed to serve him. He still does not get it that the reign of God works differently, that the order of privilege that he and others like him have created does not exist. He does not get it that his privilege is contrary to the order of God's creation. It is this obstinate clinging to a set of values that favors him over others, this lack of conscience that the constructs of privilege created in him. The perspectives and myths he adopted that he still could not let go of—what arrogance clouds his understanding. He is not able to grasp reality differently, away from meritocracy, classism, patriarchy. He had so much talent, perhaps many degrees, for what? Not even hell could help him let go. The lies are so comfortable within us. What a cozy dwelling place they have within us; they usurp the place that God's love would have within us. We are not able to respond to others as human beings with dignity. We are not able to become servants to those who for so long have served us sacrificially— the ones who have picked and who pick our crops, who wash our dishes, who cook our meals, who deliver them to our doorsteps, who clean up our human waste and bodies when we are in the hospital. We could go on with the list. In the *basileia* they are counted as great for they have served. In the end, the rich man asks: "'Then I beg you, father [Abraham], send Lazarus to my father's house [give him a nice tip], for I have five brothers. Let him warn them, so that they will not also come to this place of torment.' Abraham replied, 'They have Moses and the Prophets; let them listen to them.' [They have theological degrees]. 'No, father Abraham,' he said, 'but if someone from the dead goes to them, they will repent.' He said to him, 'If they do not listen to Moses and the

---

16. Viera, "Sermon." Insights and references from the sermon follow.

Prophets [if they do not listen to the word], they will not be convinced even if someone rises from the dead'" (Luke 16:27–31).

The word and its knowledge have been a central theme of Evangelicals but are we able to listen to the word, to the truth? What is truth in the midst of lies made to be the truth? Can we still tell the difference? The myths we live by cannot be confused with the word of God which reveals the will of God.

My sisters and my brothers, why do I speak of letting go of privilege? Because if we are faithful to the truth, reconstruction will mean that we cannot continue at the center but that we will move to the margins with the powerless ones who are at the margins. In her talk at the Center for Pastor Theologians conference, Kristin Kobes Du Mez explained the details of how we have centered ourselves.[17] It has been about marketing and becoming a part of the consumer culture. Reconstruction means decentering—the broken bones reset.

Orlando Costas does a reading of Heb 13:11–14.[18] The temple was where the blood of sacrifices was poured out, but outside the gate was where the carcasses were buried. Jesus's sacrifice takes place outside the gate. Jesus relocates worship, salvation, and mission to where the outcasts, the disenfranchised are; he is present in weakness to banish powerlessness. To reconstruct, we go out to where Jesus invites us and his Spirit is already at work. Reconstruction occupies us in the work of justice/righteousness, a realignment with God's will, for this is how we exalt his name and declare his glory—not ours—among the nations. At the center, we have substituted his glory for ours. When the church trades God's glory for its own, it seeks power, manipulation, and fame, and those who look to us will exchange the seeking of God to looking for idols. To reenter into the glory of God, we decenter through obedience and compassion, sharing of the Word that becomes in us and in our midst the true, the good, and the just. This is an incarnated word. Reconstruction is justice, compassion, responsible obedience, and incarnational fruit-bearing as disciples of Christ that glorify God.

Bibliography

Costas, Orlando E. *Christ Outside the Gate: Mission Beyond Christendom*. Maryknoll, NY: Orbis, 1982.

———. "Pecado y salvación en América Latina." In *Quito América Latina y la evangelización en los años 80: Un Congreso Auspiciado por la Fraternidad teología Latinoamericana: CLADE II, Congreso Latinoamericano de Evangelización, Noviembre de 1979*, edited by Pedro Savage and Rolando Gutierrez, 271–87. México: Fraternidad Teológica Latinoamericana, 1980.

17. Du Mez, "Which Evangelicalism."
18. See Costas, *Christ Outside the Gate*.

———. "La vida en el Espíritu." *Boletín Teológico* 21–22 (1986) 105–12.
Du Mez, Kristin Kobes. "Which Evangelicalism, Whose Purpose, and Why Even Bother?" Lecture presented at the 7th annual Theology Conference of the Center for Pastor Theologians, Oak Park, Illinois, October 2022. https://centerforpastortheologians.vhx.tv/packages/reconstructing-evangelicalism/videos/session-2-kristin-kobes-du-mez-1.
Escobar, Samuel. *Liberation Themes in Reformational Perspectives*. Sioux Center, IA: Dordt College Press, 1989.
———. "Vivir el Evangelio." *Certeza* 65 (1977) 11–13.
Heaney, Sharon. *Contextual Theology for Latin America: Liberation Themes in Evangelical Perspective*. Paternoster Theological Monographs. Eugene, OR: Wipf & Stock, 2008.
Moore, Russell. "Have Evangelicals Who Support Trump Lost Their Values?" *New York Times*, September 17, 2015. https://www.nytimes.com/2015/09/17/opinion/have-evangelicals-who-support-trump-lost-their-values.html.
Smith, Gregory A. "Among White Evangelicals, Regular Churchgoers Are the Most Supportive of Trump." *Pew Research Center*, April 26, 2017. http://www.pewresearch.org/fact-tanl/2017/04/26/among-white-evangelicals-regular-churchgoers-are-the-most-supportive-of-trump/.
Swanson, David W. *Rediscipling the White Church: From Cheap Diversity to True Solidarity*. Downers Grove, IL: IVP, 2020.
Tisby, Jemar. *The Color of Compromise: The Truth About the American Church's Complicity in Racism*. Grand Rapids: Zondervan Reflective, 2019.
Viera, Javier. "Sermon." AETH Biennial Meeting, October 20, 2022.
Wink, Walter. *Naming the Powers*. Philadelphia: Fortress, 1984.

4

In Search of "Biblical" Masculinity

Today's Crisis of Masculinity

ZACHARY WAGNER

Introduction

THERE MAY BE BROAD agreement that our society is facing a crisis of masculinity,[1] but disagreement abounds as to the nature of the crisis, its causes, and the proposed solutions. Is this crisis manifesting in the number of men and boys who experience aimlessness, joblessness, or who fail to succeed in school? Is it caused by the ascendence of women into more and more positions of leadership in society? Is the popularity of video games to blame? Or the advent of free access porn and high-speed internet? Is fatherlessness the cause of the crisis or a result of it? Or both? Is the loss of traditional male role models impoverishing boys and men's imaginations of who they might become?

Answering these questions is well beyond the scope of this chapter, much less my expertise or insight. But closer to home for me and the readers of this volume will be the current crisis and confusion around men and masculinity in the church. A slew of recent books by women authors, scholars, and historians has precipitated a discussion of the malformation of men and the problems of sexual abuse and male abuses of power in the church.[2] Evangelicals did

---

1. A masculine crisis of some form or another has long been prophesied about and against, e.g. Horrocks, *Masculinity in Crisis*. More recently, see Reeves, *Of Boys and Men*.

2. These include such books as James, *Malestrom*; Byrd, *Recovering from Biblical*

not invent "toxic" masculinity, but Christians of all traditions are responsible for the manifestations of abusive and dehumanizing attitudes and behaviors in their communities. A laundry list of scandals and allegations would quickly consume this chapter's allotted word count, and more and more scandals appear to be unearthed with the passing weeks and months.

If Christian masculinity is broken, the natural and sincere question for many well-meaning pastors and congregants becomes, "What vision of masculinity is commended in the Bible?" In this chapter I hope to offer a fresh approach to this question for evangelical pastors, theologians, and congregants. For the second half of the chapter, I will also offer more focused reflections on a Christian vision of male sexuality.

Traditional or Disruptive? Evaluating the Biblical Evidence

What is the Bible's vision of and for masculinity? This question touches on an ongoing debate among some New Testament (NT) scholars as to whether early Christian "masculinities" were hegemonic—i.e., conforming to or affirming mainstream political and cultural values—or subversive—i.e., undermining and re-envisioning masculinity against those values.[3] Perhaps another, though admittedly anachronistic, way of framing this question is whether the NT commends a masculinity that is traditional or progressive.[4] Of course, when we ask whether the Bible supports "traditional" masculinity, this raises the question: traditional relative to what/where/whom? The masculine values and ideals of any culture are not homogeneous, and there was no single standard ideal of masculinity in the ancient world any more than there is one in modern America. While certain concepts of masculinity are common across time and cultures, the concept of "true" manliness is wildly diverse. Thus, it is important to note that what modern readers associate with manliness may not map directly onto the world in which the biblical authors were writing.

Manhood and Womanhood. In 2020 and 2021, two historical treatments rose to prominence, namely Barr, *Making of Biblical Womanhood*, and Du Mez, *Jesus and John Wayne*, the latter of which reached the *New York Times* bestseller list.

3. For a helpful recent overview, see Conway, "Masculinity Studies." See also Haddox, "Favoured Sons."

4. This is a loose usage of these terms that I hope serves my argument rather than proves distracting. What I mean by "traditional" is merely a reference to masculine values that are received and valued from a previous or series of previous generations. What I mean by progressive is merely a "new" or nontraditional vision of masculinity, not necessarily one that represents social progress toward some goal.

To illustrate this point, we can make some generalizations about Greco-Roman masculine values. By almost any modern standard, the ancient world was unflinchingly misogynistic and patriarchal, as illustrated by a quote from Diogenes, "Thales . . . [said] there were three blessings for which he was grateful to Fortune: 'First, that I was born a human being and not one of the brutes; next, that I was born a man and not a woman; thirdly, a Greek and not a barbarian.'"[5] In both Greek and Roman culture, virtue was closely associated with manliness. (Hence the Latin word for virtue, *virtus*, is derived from the word for man, *vir*.) Elite masculinity, most fundamentally, entailed self-control or self-mastery,[6] but this clearly extended to control over *others*. In an imagined dialogue between Alexander the Great and his father Philip, the first-century orator Dio Chrysostom writes that being a real man means being a "master of all."[7] Femininity, by contrast, was often associated with the passions, irrationality, subservience, and submission. It was also associated in many cases with vice. To give one example, Seneca, a first-century Roman stoic, writes, "anger is a most womanish and childish weakness."[8] Comments such as this undermine just how different gender association between our own day and the ancient world can be, even while we may find some overlap between them.

The ancient dominance-centric vision of masculinity, for instance, extended in ways that both do and do not correspond to today's concepts of the masculine. Unsurprisingly, warriors and military heroes were held in high regard, especially those who were given command over others and led the armies. However, while agriculture was seen by some as a noble enterprise, it was the *supervision* and oversight of the manual labor that was considered most manly. The men doing what we might consider the "real work" in the fields would have been understood as servile (they were, after all, slaves in many cases) and, for this reason, less manly. Working with your hands was sometimes considered *unmasculine* because real men can exert enough power and control over others that they will do their work for them. Thus, our

---

5. Diogenes, *Thales* 1.33. Cf. Dio Chrysostom: "[Y]ou see that God has everywhere appointed the superior to care for and rule over the inferior: skill, for instance, over unskilfulness, strength over weakness. . . . Then compare the lots of man and woman. Now everyone would admit that man is stronger than woman and more fitted to lead." Dio Chrysostom, *Kingship* 3.62, 70.

6. See a brief summary discussion in Glancy, "Protocols of Masculinity," 240–41. See also a helpful overview of the early history of virtue as self-mastery in Taylor, *Sources of the Self*, 115–26. See also Conway, *Behold the Man*, 15–34.

7. Dio Chrysostom, *Kingship* 2.6–7.

8. Seneca, *Ira* 20.3.

masculine values of hard, physical labor do not neatly map onto the ancient world, at least not without significant qualification.

The question "What does it mean to be a man?" does not have a consistent answer throughout history. Indeed, throughout American history the vision of ideal manhood has itself adapted and changed, as a historical overview like Michael Kimmel's *Manhood in America* demonstrates.[9] These factors complicate the questions of how "biblical" masculinity relates to other potential visions of masculinity in our day. It would be one thing if the biblical text included lengthy treatises describing masculinity or what it means to be a "true man," but it does not. If one were to identify central themes of the Bible, manliness, I would argue, would not rank high on that list. This is, of course, part of the point. It is not that the Bible has nothing to say to men about how they should live *as men*. It does. But manliness is not the same thing as "godliness." And it is important for Christians and pastors to acknowledge that the data from which we can reconstruct an "ideal" biblical masculinity is somewhat sparse. This raises the question as to whether it is a wise thing to attempt in the first place, a question we will return to at the conclusion of this chapter. Now, we turn to the biblical text itself.

Hegemonic and Disruptive Biblical Masculinity

Do the biblical authors anywhere seem to affirm the values and virtues associated with masculinity in the ancient world? The short answer is yes, but it's complicated. If we are looking for traditional, strong, masculine motifs in Scripture, we can find them. For instance, manly warrior tropes are common in the Old Testament's historical narratives. Joshua is told to "be strong and courageous" (Josh 1:9 NIV). In 1 Samuel, David is introduced as a handsome, fearless, and valiant warrior. In the NT, Jesus's crucifixion could quite naturally be interpreted as a heroic sacrifice for the good of his people and friends (John 15:13), potentially modelling a masculine mode of self-sacrifice recognizable in both the ancient world and today. Moreover, Jesus's appearance at the conclusion of Revelation is as a conquering warrior, riding on a white horse, ostensibly ready to slaughter his enemies with a sword from his mouth (Rev 19:11–16). Among the virtue lists and exhortations in the Pauline epistles and beyond we see such charges as "be strong" (ἀνδρίζεσθε, 1 Cor 16:13), a lengthy description of putting on armor for spiritual warfare (Eph 6:10–18) and the reminder that the faith-filled of old became powerful in battle and put enemy armies to flight (Heb 11:32–35).

---

9. Kimmel, *Manhood in America*.

But warrior tropes are not the only traditional masculine values we find. In the Pastoral Epistles, men who are successful heads of house are seen as natural candidates for eldership (1 Tim 3:4–5). Since they have demonstrated the capacity to manage and direct the behavior of a smaller house (i.e., their children), presumably they will be able to do the same in "God's household." Jennifer Glancy writes, in setting out the qualifications for elders, Paul "implicitly specifies norms for the behavior of mature Christian men." This is because a natural assumption is that the best, noblest—and thus, most "manly"—men were destined to be rulers and leaders in the ancient world. Glancy goes on, "many of these [qualifications] are associated with properly self-controlled masculinity in pagan writings of the era."[10] However, Glancy overstates the case when she claims that "the Pastoral Epistles serve as a Christian hornbook of masculine propriety."[11] That the letter to Timothy includes virtue exhortations is beyond dispute, but that these virtues are gendered and oriented toward manliness in particular is less clear. This is complicated by the fact that virtue was so closely associated with manliness in the ancient world—any type of virtue, particularly virtues of self-control, will have a masculine "feel" to scholars of the ancient world. And while the recipients and primary audience of the pastoral epistles are ostensibly men, the letters are not charged with *explicitly* gendered language.[12] The Pastorals also include exhortations for women (Titus 2:3–5), and presumably, even in the first and early second century, women would have felt that they too were included in such an exhortation as, "Flee the evil desires of youth and pursue righteousness, faith, love and peace, along with those who call on the Lord out of a pure heart" (2 Tim 2:22 NIV).

Alongside the hegemonic biblical examples given above, we also find regular representations of and exhortations toward what masculinity studies have sometimes called "disruptive" masculinities. For instance, the patriarchal narratives of Genesis repeatedly demonstrate that God does not always favor the most masculine men, but rather those men who "model a proper relationship with God."[13] Perhaps the most striking example of this is God's election of Jacob, the brother who favors cooking and spending time with his mother, over Esau, his hairy, hunter, twin brother. This narrative is an early example of a pattern we see throughout the Hebrew Bible as well as the NT, namely that God delights in "reversals"[14] and chooses the apparently weak to demonstrate

---

10. Glancy, "Protocols of Masculinity," 237–38.
11. Glancy, "Protocols of Masculinity," 237.
12. For a contrasting series of treatises on virtue that *do* contain gendered language, see Dio Chrysostom's discourses on kingship, *Kingship* 1–4.
13. Haddox, "Favoured Sons," 15.
14. Lee-Barnewall and Cohick, *Neither Complementarian*, 77–81.

his power through them. We see a further example of this pattern in how God describes his election of Israel in Deut 7:7, "The Lord did not set his affection on you and choose you because you were more numerous than other peoples, for you were the fewest of all peoples" (NIV).

When there is fighting to be done in the Scriptures, the narrative emphasis often falls on the fact that the fighting is done by Yahweh on the people's behalf. Repeatedly, God tells his people that *he* will fight for them, and they will be victorious despite their weakness. As Pharoah and his chariots are closing in against the people at the Red Sea, Moses tells them, "Do not be afraid. Stand firm and you will see the deliverance the Lord will bring you today. The Egyptians you see today you will never see again. The Lord will fight for you; you need only to be still" (Exod 14:13–14 NIV). This is also powerfully illustrated when Gideon gathers his men for battle and Yahweh tells him, "You have too many men. I cannot deliver Midian into their hands, or Israel would boast against me, 'My own strength has saved me'" (Judg 7:2 NIV). After whittling down his army, Gideon is left with three hundred men, only 1.5 percent of his original twenty-two thousand. Despite this, Gideon and his army miraculously prevail over the Midianites.

Saul, Israel's first king, is a head taller than all the other men (1 Sam 9:2)—a trait strongly implied to be *negative* because it is reminiscent of the description of the Canaanites who were "strong" with "fortified and very large cities" (Num 13:28 ESV) and very tall (Num 13:32–33, cf. Amos 2:9). When Samuel prepares to anoint one of the sons of Jesse as the new king over Israel, God rebukes him for assuming an older brother is to be anointed (presumably because of his appearance). Yahweh says, "Do not consider his appearance or his height, for I have rejected him. The Lord does not look at the things people look at. People look at the outward appearance, but the Lord looks at the heart" (1 Sam 16:7 NIV).

These masculine-subversive themes show up elsewhere. The warlike nations surrounding Israel are regularly *condemned* for what one might describe as their hyper-masculinity. The psalmists give voice not only to courage and resolve, but also to weakness, confusion, and fear in the face of one's enemies (e.g., Ps 6:6–7). The hope of the psalmist is that *God* will turn back his enemies, not that the psalmist himself will double down on his strength and manliness and put them to flight himself (Ps 6:8–9). Another form of reversal appearing in the Hebrew Bible is that of women who transgress gender norms when they take on and step into assumed male "roles," such as the prophet and judge, Deborah. In the book of Ruth, it is Ruth, taking advice from her mother-in-law, who boldly initiates a match with Boaz by going to the threshing floor (Ruth 3:1–14).

Potentially disruptive versions of masculinity also appear in the NT. Jesus's ministry is marked by association with the vulnerable and uninfluential. The beatitudes emphasize decidedly unmasculine characteristics such as meekness, poverty of spirit, and humiliation through persecution (Matt 5:3–12). When Peter rises (heroically?) to protect Jesus from being arrested, Jesus rebukes him and tells him to put his sword away (Matt 26:52; John 18:11). We noted above that one way to read Jesus's crucifixion was as a heroic sacrifice—which it certainly was. However, another reading arguably more natural in the ancient world would have been that Jesus was emasculated by his suffering and crucifixion.[15] He willingly submitted to a total loss of bodily autonomy, subjected himself to the shame of being beaten and penetrated in the crucifixion itself.[16] The very mode of execution was designed to be maximally humiliating and emasculating, such that a crucified messiah would have been a contradiction in terms.[17]

The Hebrew Bible and NT's consistent taboos against same-sex eroticism and sexual immorality stood in stark contrast to Greco-Roman assumption that powerful men were entitled to sexual domination of their inferiors (whether women, other men, or boys) so long as doing so did not transgress another man's household or property. However, while the NT holds heterosexual marriage in high regard, it also at times undermines masculine ideals associated with sexuality and marriage. In Matt 19:12, Jesus speaks of those who have made themselves eunuchs for the kingdom of heaven. Whether this is a reference to literal emasculation or not, it certainly undermines a masculine ideal wherein *all* Christian men must prove their worth by taking a wife. Indeed, the ministries of Jesus and Paul themselves undermine this ideal, since both were single, celibate men. Leading a household never rises to the level of a Christian masculine imperative. Even in the household codes of Eph 5 and 1 Pet 3, the emphasis for husbands falls not on "leadership" or dominance, but instead on love, respect, and self-sacrifice.

Finally, the NT authors paradoxically elevate weakness, even servanthood, as noble—a moral charge that would have been antithetical to masculine Roman values. Jesus says that "the last will be first" (Matt 20:16 NIV) and the "meek . . . will inherit the earth" (Matt 5:5 NIV) He says of himself that "the Son of Man did not come to be served, but to serve" (Mark 10:45 NIV). Paul similarly teaches that "God chose the weak things of the world to shame the strong" (1 Cor 1:27 NIV). He identifies himself as a servant, both of

---

15. So argued by Glancy, "Protocols of Masculinity," 263. Cf. Origen, *Against Celsus*, 7.53–55.

16. Cf. Phil 2:8; Heb 12:2.

17. Cf. 1 Cor 1:23.

Christ (Rom 1:1) and of the people in his congregations (1 Cor 9:19); justifies his unimposing, sickly appearance (2 Cor 10:10); and boasts in his weakness (2 Cor 12:9). Paul's arguments and illustrations include gendered imagery that is a mix of male and female domains, wherein he can both employ and rework gender stereotypes to suit the rhetorical or theological point he is making.[18]

Where Are the "Strong" Biblical Men?

To return to our original question—does the Bible affirm or reject traditional modes of masculinity? The answer, it seems, is both. The biblical authors, on the whole, do not have a neatly hegemonic nor a uniformly subversive vision of masculinity—whether relative to the ancient world or the modern West. For every text that valorizes manliness and strength, we might find another that relativizes and marginalizes what we consider manly. Does this mean the Bible is incoherent in its vision of masculinity? Perhaps not. I see two alternate and related conclusions that we might draw. First, proof-texting "biblical masculinity" is not a responsible approach, and doing so runs the risk of adapting our selection of texts to suit what we already believe masculinity should look like. Second, the entire enterprise of searching for "biblical masculinity" may be misguided in the sense that encouraging men to be more manly is not an emphasis of Jesus or the apostles' ministry.

We will have to ask deeper, more challenging, and potentially uncomfortable questions of the biblical text if we hope to hear the Spirit's word to Christian men today. And here is where a pastor theologian has, it seems to me, work to do. Too often the pursuit of becoming a godly man becomes more about being manly than it is about being godly. The disentangling of cultural values of masculinity from biblical texts will be delicate and challenging work for many boys and men, often challenging their assumptions about what Christian manhood must look like. Since, both in the ancient world and in our own, manliness is so closely associated with strength, we should bear close to mind as a church how the Bible—and, indeed, the gospel—undermines a strength-centric ethic and worldview. These are not the only masculine associations that may need reevaluation. Some of the popular tenets of so-called "biblical manhood" do not hold up under closer scriptural scrutiny. For instance, the buzzword "spiritual leadership"—the supposed role of men in the home—appears nowhere in Scripture. What is more, men are nowhere in Scripture explicitly told to *lead* their wives, but rather to *love* their wives (e.g.,

---

18. Westfall, *Paul and Gender*, 45–59.

Eph 5:25; Col 3:19).[19] Bible-believing Christians and Bible-teaching pastors and ministers need to think and speak much more carefully about what the Bible does and does not teach about manhood, subjecting our assumptions and beliefs—even our "traditional" ones—to careful scrutiny, as well as historical and cultural critique. For the remainder of this chapter, I will attempt to model this approach with a discussion of male sexuality.

Sexual Abuse and the Revising of Masculine Norms[20]

As we consider the topic of deconstruction and whether, how, and if we can *reconstruct* Evangelicalism, it is worth considering what the common reasons for deconstruction are. For many young Christians and former Christians, questions and issues of sexuality stand out among the others. As recent abuse crises have brought to the fore, sexual abuse and misconduct among Christian men and male Christian leaders is alarmingly common, and steps taken to address and prevent it are often minimal or even nonexistent. Though some may interpret the exposure of these scandals and the fall of these leaders and organizations as a sign of a spiritual attack by Satan, my read is that this is, quite clearly, a judgment of God *against* evangelical hypocrisy. Aptly, Russell Moore referred to a report on abuse within the Southern Baptist Convention as a "Southern Baptist apocalypse."[21]

Evangelicalism has a male sexuality problem, and perhaps the problem is not that either men, the church, or the culture is not masculine enough. It may be, instead, that we have adopted an unbiblical, ahistorical, theologically weak, sub-Christian, indeed *anti*-Christian vision of what it means to be male. Too often our responses to crises and scandals of sexual abuse are reactive rather than proactive. Yes, we should quickly and decisively take the institutional and legal steps necessary to hold Christian abusers to account and care for the victims of their abuses of power. But beyond this, we must ask what vision of masculine sexuality gives rise to these abuses.

A masculine characteristic that is often taken for granted both inside and outside the church is that men are helplessly and hopelessly hypersexual. The extremely popular *Every Man's Battle* series codifies this vision of maleness

---

19. At best, the call to leadership is an assumption implied by the charge that women should submit to their husbands. Debates on these texts are voluminous, of course. My only point here is one of stress and emphasis. The center of "biblical" husbanding is not leadership; it is love.

20. See Wagner, *Non-Toxic Masculinity*, for a further development of many of the ideas in this section.

21. Moore, "This Is the Southern Baptist Apocalypse."

in the title itself. Much of our ways of speaking about male sexuality in the church presents the constant "battle" against sexual sin as an inevitable part of being male. Ironically, this stereotypes and often forms men *toward* hypersexualization rather than away from it. For men, it is argued, lust is an inevitable problem to be managed, and the temptation to objectify others for erotic gratification is simply "part of being a guy." This sets the bar terrifyingly low for men; we have adopted and normalized an immature hypersexual view of maleness and masculinity. The discipleship programs coming out of this vision too often focus on preventative measures to control and restrain men's lusts, fixating on creating boundaries rather than helping men grow in maturity. For instance, strict accountability parameters like the so-called Billy Graham Rule[22] sexualize (in a heteronormative lens) *all* relationships. Insistence that male leaders cannot travel alone imply that no man can be trusted alone. If a man goes to a hotel, is it somehow inevitable that he's going to hire a prostitute or watch porn all night?

If these and other related teachings are said to have a biblical warrant, perhaps it would be taken from the various instructions on sex, marriage, and singleness in 1 Cor 7. In churches today, sexually frustrated young men are told to pursue a marriage relationship in order to have a God-sanctioned "outlet" for their sexual urges. On a certain level this may seem like sound advice, but Paul's very contextualized instructions in 1 Corinthians should not be overread as a principle for how to deal with immature sexuality. First, the language is not gendered. Paul does not say, "since men struggle to stay sexually pure, they should get married and wives should not deprive their husbands." Marriage is not held out in this passage as an erotic paradise in which no man will ever need to bear up under temptation to sexual sin. Indeed, simply being married is no guarantee of automatic or lasting sexual "satisfaction." A superficial understanding of this passage, isolated from the rest of the witness of Scripture, commodifies sex and removes it from relational context. Marriage is not merely a mechanism for having sex in a way that God approves of. Too often the radical mutuality of 1 Cor 7 is reduced to a scriptural club that immature men use to coerce and assault their wives. This is horrific and reprehensible. Too often Christian men are not told to tame their hyper sexuality. They are told instead to control and redirect it toward marriage. A wife then becomes the release valve for a man's dehumanizing urges, his own personal porn star.

By contrast, the NT vision of male sexuality demands sexual holiness and assumes that men are in fact capable of chaste and virtuous living. It charges

---

22. Which teaches that a man and a woman who are not married to each other should avoid ever spending time alone in a room or a car with a member of the opposite sex.

men to treat women like sisters in all purity (1 Tim 5:2), not to view them as threats or dehumanize them by sexually objectifying them through avoidance. Access to sex in marriage is not the only or even the primary mechanism by which men should strive toward sexual integrity and maturity. For instance, Jesus's charge that the man who looks at a woman with lust in his heart has already committed adultery with her does not mean that men should never look at women. Rather, it means that it is incumbent on men to look at women *differently*. A discipleship structure that holds out marriage as the solution to a man's every sexual frustration is profoundly dehumanizing, both for men and for women.

As Evangelicals, we should pause and ask what is shaping our imagination around masculinity. Is it Scripture or the masculine values of the world? Recall that the Apostle Paul charges believers not to be conformed to the pattern of this world—and the world has normalized the objectification and dehumanization of women. Christians should be participating in a new world where this is no longer the case.

Conclusions and Final Reflections

In the ancient world, it would have been problematic for apostles and church leaders to, in an unqualified way, exhort believers to be "manly." This is because there were many masculine values in that world that were contrary to the new humanity being made in Christ. The same is no doubt true today. Manliness, by our cultural conception, is sometimes at odds with Christian virtue. This is certainly the case as it relates to male stereotypes around sexuality, which conceive of men as out-of-control sex machines. When Christians adopt such a view, men's discipleship becomes a matter of lust management.

Christianity does not abolish masculinity; it redefines what it means to be a virtuous man. It does this, for instance, by downplaying the value of physical strength or the centrality of eroticism in the male experience. Christian men (and Christians in general) should avoid sexual immorality, idolatry, hatred, discord, jealousy, fits of rage, selfish ambition, dissensions, factions and envy, drunkenness, orgies, and the like. On the contrary, they should be filled by God's Spirit with love, joy, peace, patience, kindness, goodness, faithfulness, gentleness, and self-control (Gal 6:19–25). As Christians, we ultimately get our ethical cues not from cultural standards but from the new world being witnessed to by Jesus and the apostles' teaching about the Kingdom of God. But the Bible, in my view, does more than redefine manliness; it *decenters* masculinity from our formational priorities. Christian virtue, the imitation of Christ, is not gendered.

That the Bible does not bow to cultural standards of masculinity is good news for men for several reasons. It frees men from the endless grind of proving your masculine worth to the world. A man need not attain other men's standard of manliness to be received as a beloved and valued son of God and heir to his kingdom. Men who do not fit the manly standards of the culture or even the church—whether by temperament, disposition, physical constitution, libido—are dignified when they see that Christ himself was willing to be emasculated by the cultural standards of his day. In Christ, men are called to become their fully alive and virtuous selves, the men they were created to be, *whether or not* they measure up to culturally situated standards of being a "real" man.[23]

Living like this is sometimes humiliating, and at times it may feel *unmasculine*. But that is the point of the cross: that God chose the weak and wimpy things of the world to put the powers of the world to shame. Our discipleship of men should conform to the scandal and, yes, the ironic triumph of the cross. Such a discipleship paradigm will exhort men not just toward manliness, but toward maturity. A maturity that does not need to be superficially understood as manly to know that we are valued and loved by God. A maturity that is willing to put up with sexual frustration and humiliation without using it as an excuse for dehumanizing others or indulging in sin. A maturity that sets down worldly power in pursuit of peace and justice.

Bibliography

Barr, Beth Allison. *The Making of Biblical Womanhood: How the Subjugation of Women Became Gospel Truth*. Grand Rapids, MI: Brazos, 2021.

Byrd, Aimee. *Recovering from Biblical Manhood and Womanhood: How the Church Needs to Rediscover Her Purpose*. Grand Rapids: Zondervan, 2020.

Conway, Colleen M. *Behold the Man: Jesus and Greco-Roman Masculinity*. Oxford: Oxford University Press, 2008.

———. "Masculinity Studies." In *The Oxford Handbook of New Testament, Gender, and Sexuality*, edited by Benjamin H. Dunning, 77–94. Oxford: Oxford University Press, 2019.

Du Mez, Kristin Kobes. *Jesus and John Wayne: How White Evangelicals Corrupted a Faith and Fractured a Nation*. New York: W. W. Norton, 2020.

Glancy, Jennifer A. "Protocols of Masculinity in the Pastoral Epistles." In *New Testament Masculinities*, edited by Stephen D. Moore and Janice Capel Anderson, 235–64. Semeia Studies 45. Atlanta: Society of Biblical Literature, 2003.

Haddox, Susan. "Favoured Sons and Subordinate Masculinities." In *Men and Masculinity in the Hebrew Bible and Beyond*, edited by Ovidiu Creangă, 2–17. Bible in the Modern World 33. Sheffield: Phoenix, 2010.

---

23. See Pearcy, *Toxic War on Masculinity*.

PART ONE: CHALLENGES

Horrocks, Roger. *Masculinity in Crisis: Myths, Fantasies and Realities*. Basingstoke: Macmillan, 1994.

James, Carolyn Custis. *Malestrom: Manhood Swept into the Currents of a Changing World*. Grand Rapids: Zondervan, 2015.

Kimmel, Michael S. *Manhood in America: A Cultural History*. New York: Free, 1996.

Lee-Barnewall, Michelle, and Lynn Cohick. *Neither Complementarian nor Egalitarian: A Kingdom Corrective to the Evangelical Gender Debate*. Grand Rapids: Baker Academic, 2016.

Moore, Russell. "This Is the Southern Baptist Apocalypse." *Christianity Today*, May 22, 2022. https://www.christianitytoday.com/ct/2022/may-web-only/southern-baptist-abuse-apocalypse-russell-moore.html.

Moore, Stephen D. "'O Man, Who Art Thou . . . ?': Masculinity Studies and New Testament Studies." In *New Testament Masculinities*, edited by Stephen D. Moore and Janice Capel Anderson, 1–22. Semeia Studies 45. Atlanta: Society of Biblical Literature, 2003.

Pearcy, Nancy. *The Toxic War on Masculinity: How Christianity Reconciles the Sexes*. Grand Rapids: Baker, 2023.

Reeves, Richard V. *Of Boys and Men: Why the Modern Male Is Struggling, Why It Matters, and What to Do about It*. London: Swift, 2022.

Taylor, Charles. *Sources of the Self: The Making of the Modern Identity*. Cambridge: Harvard University Press, 1992.

Wagner, Zachary. *Non-Toxic Masculinity: Recovering Healthy Male Sexuality*. Downers Grove, IL: IVP, 2023.

Westfall, Cynthia Long. *Paul and Gender: Reclaiming the Apostle's Vision for Men and Women in Christ*. Grand Rapids: Baker Academic, 2016.

5

Evangelicalism in Nigeria

A Bowl of Mixed Fruits

BABATUNDE OLADIMEJI

INTRODUCTION

IN AFRICA, WE SPEAK of the need to have different ingredients and condiments in order to do good cooking. This belief is also seen when you choose fruits; we are encouraged to mix sweet and bitter herbs and fruits to get the best mix for healthy living. The questions we pose are this: is it possible to take the various expressions of Evangelicalism in Africa as a plate of mixed fruits? If so, what might we take out to make Evangelicalism a better mix? Is it possible for us to deconstruct and then reconstruct Evangelicalism in Africa? What are the essential features that would be needed to achieve this endeavor, so that we could have a balance of mixed fruits?

ORIGIN OF THE EVANGELICALS

The origin of the Evangelicals can be traced back to 1738 and was influenced by a number of religious movements contributing to its foundation, including pietism, radical pietism, Quakerism, Presbyterianism, and Moravianism (in particular its bishop Nicolaus Zinzendorf and his community at Herrnhut). During the first Great Awakening, John Wesley and other early Methodists were primarily responsible for igniting this new movement. Evangelicals can now be found in numerous Protestant branches as well as in different faiths that are not part of any one specific branch. Nicolaus Zinzendorf, George Fox, John Wesley, George Whitefield, Jonathan Edwards, Billy Graham, and Harold Ockenga—among many others—were among the leaders and major figures of the evangelical movement.

The movement had a presence in the Anglosphere, gaining great momentum during the time period of the Great Awakenings in Great Britain and the United States, before spreading further in the nineteenth, twentieth, and early twenty-first centuries. In 2016, it was estimated that 619 million Evangelicals were in the world, meaning that one in four Christians would be classified as evangelical. Based on this research, it was discovered that the United States has the largest portion of the Evangelicals in the world. American Evangelicals are a quarter of that nation's population and its single largest religious group.

Nigeria: A Leader in African Christianity

Nigeria is the most populous country in Africa. It is situated on the Gulf of Guinea in West Africa. Its neighbors are Benin, Niger, Cameroon, and Chad. The lower course of the river Niger flows south through the western part of the country into the Gulf of Guinea. Swamps and mangrove forests border the southern coast; inland are hardwood forests. It is also surrounded on the southern side by the Atlantic Ocean and in the north by the Sahara Desert.[1]

The capital city is Abuja, while the commercial city is Lagos, which is also the tenth most populous city in the world. Land area is 351,649 square miles, and the total area is 356,667 square miles. The population according to the World Factbook of the Central Intelligence Agency is 162,470,737 in 2011, including more than two hundred and fifty ethnic groups, such as the Hausa and Fulani at 29 percent, Yoruba at 21 percent, Igbo at 18 percent, Jaw at 10 percent, Kanuri at 4.9 percent, Ibibio at 3.5 percent, and Tiv at 2.5 percent. The official language is English, but more than five hundred other indigenous languages are also used.[2]

The Christian church in Nigeria has become a major force in global Christianity. Nigeria has produced several highly influential figures in Christianity. The Anglican church, being the first church to be successfully established in Nigeria, has continued to generate its own influence in global Anglicanism because of its vibrancy and growth. Some of the largest church buildings of

---

1. Central Intelligence Agency, "People and Society." Current figures put the population much higher.

2. Central Intelligence Agency, "People and Society."

other denominations are in Nigeria, with some of the largest numbers of worshippers. For example, the Redeemed Christian Church of God in Nigeria, which started seventy years ago, has churches in over one hundred and ninety countries of the world. The Winners Chapel has one of the largest church buildings in the world with branches in many African countries and other parts of the world. Salvation Ministries has quite a lot of churches too, with Dunamis International Church, a 100,000-seater church in Abuja, regularly hosting programs in many countries in Africa.

The advent of Christianity in Nigeria emerged in different phases depending on which denominational approach one takes. The consensus is that it was largely driven by the missionary endeavor of the Church Missionary Society of the Church of England and the Methodist Church. The movement into Badagry and Egbaland in southwestern Nigeria between 1839 and 1842 was the key to the sustaining work of mission in Nigeria. The labors of Thomas Freedman and Henry Townsend, along with the extensive work of Ajayi Crowther, became the foundation for the planting of Christianity in Nigeria.[3]

Evangelicalism on the Continent

It is critical that we understand what Evangelicalism means on the African continent. Anthony Balcomb opines that "Evangelicalism in Africa should be understood more by what it does for its adherents than by its doctrinal formulations. Its success on the subcontinent of Africa could be due to the fact that it transacts at the interface of a modern and pre-modern worldview."[4] We therefore should take note that Africans certainly define Evangelicalism differently.

The Association of Evangelicals in Africa (AEA) was founded in 1966, with headquarters in Nairobi, Kenya. Registered as a charitable organization and presently comprising forty national evangelical fellowships as full members, it is one of the regional associations of the global evangelical movement—the World Evangelical Alliance (WEA).[5]

According to their documents, a few key beliefs in their statement of faith include the infallibility of Scripture and its supreme authority in all matters of faith and conduct. Next is the indwelling of the Holy Spirit in the believer in

---

3. See Komolafe, *Transformation of African Christianity*, 30–45.
4. Balcomb, "Evangelicalism in Africa," 117–28.
5. "Who We Are," Association of Evangelicals in Africa.

order to live a holy life and witness and work for the Lord Jesus Christ. The third is the personal existence of Satan.[6]

The association does have regional offices with presidents and secretaries for countries including Nigeria. Gordon-Cornwell Theological Seminary suggested that of the 115 million Christians in Africa, about 23 percent are Evangelical.[7] However, the AEA proposed that there are between 150 and 180 million Evangelicals in Africa.[8]

One problem that comes up with conceptualizing Evangelicalism in Africa is that most people use Western criteria as a means of defining Evangelicals worldwide. The fourfold components of Evangelicalism have been used by many: *conversionism*, which insists on personal conversion; *activism*, which is the need for the evangelization of others; *biblicism*, which is the belief in biblical inerrancy; and *crucicentrism*, which emphasizes the centrality of the cross.[9] Balcomb asserts that when people use these criteria, they are using an element of propositional value which implies that, to be an Evangelical you are to believe "in certain doctrinal verities, of the order of a statement of faith. This kind of propositionalism is typical of Western Protestantism and certainly of Western Evangelicalism."[10] But in Africa, the existential circumstances and the consequences of Evangelicalism are quite different. It will be appropriate to agree that there is some continuity between what Evangelicalism is in the West and in Africa, but in Africa it is much more than the four cardinal points of Western Evangelicalism; it is far more about what it does to and for Jesus's followers.[11] So, with this in mind, we can understand why Evangelicals in Nigeria are known for some forms of ethical standards like no drinking of alcohol, no partying, no sex before marriage, and many other things.

I am of the view that it is this important factor about what it does to and for his followers that provides Evangelicalism's strong attachment to Pentecostalism in many places in Africa and especially Nigeria. It is important to note that many of the old evangelical churches in Nigeria still maintain their core doctrines on their statement of faith and theological policies, but they have

---

6. "Who We Are," Association of Evangelicals in Africa.

7. Zurlo, "Demographics of Global Evangelicalism," 34–47.

8. Balcomb believes that this figure is an exaggeration since they are not up to this figure worldwide.

9. Bebbington, *Evangelicalism in Modern Britain*. For a more exhaustive treatment, see Sweeney, *American Evangelical Story*.

10. Balcomb, "Evangelicalism in Africa," 118.

11. Balcomb, "Evangelicalism in Africa," 118.

been fully influenced by the charismatic and Pentecostal movements, thereby changing their ecclesiastical expressions.

History of Charismatic Movement in Nigeria

There is no agreement among African scholars on who the charismatics are. Whereas some scholars such as Afe Adogame[12] use "Pentecostal" and "charismatic" interchangeably, Ogbu Kalu[13] and Matthew Ojo[14] see them as two different movements. Ojo says that the term *charismatics* is generally applied to Christians within the Protestant and Roman Catholic churches who testify to the baptism of the Holy Spirit with the evidence of speaking in tongues and the exercise of the gifts of the Holy Spirit.[15] Kalu seems to present Pentecostalism as the bigger umbrella, including the charismatics. For the purpose of this essay the term *charismatic* does not describe denominations but movements within missional churches such as the Roman Catholics, Anglicans, Methodists, and others, including the Baptists. As Kalu states, "The Charismatic goals were both to re-evangelize the mainline churches as well as to win new souls for the kingdom."[16] He observes different phases of the charismatic movement, which generally follow the earlier contributors such as Sokari Braide. The first was between 1914–38, which was not part of the Aladura movement of Moses Orimolade, Ayo Bababola, and others. This first phase, however, led to the formation of the Christ Apostolic church. The second phase included the Aladura movements of Orimolade, Oshitelu, and others. The third was in 1970 after the Nigerian Civil War.[17]

Worldwide Pentecostalism

The origin of the modern Pentecostal movement is associated with the outpouring of the Holy Spirit in Charles Fox Parham's Bible College in Topeka, Kansas, in 1901. The majority of Pentecostals, however, link Pentecostalism to the revival that began with William Seymour's Apostolic Faith Mission on Azusa Street in Los Angeles in 1906.[18] Many people came from different parts

---

12. Adogame, *Who Is Afraid of the Holy Ghost?*, xvii.
13. Kalu, *African Pentecostalism*, 359.
14. Ojo, "Charismatic Movement," 114.
15. Ojo, "Charismatic Movement," 114.
16. Kalu, *African Pentecostalism*, 88.
17. Kalu, *African Pentecostalism*, 88.
18. Albrecht, *Rites in the Spirit*, 34.

of the world to receive the experience of the Azusa Street Revival. The press also noticed the revival and published its existence throughout the whole of the United States and the world.[19] This revival produced many denominations such as the Assemblies of God and the Foursquare Gospel Church, which are mostly called classical Pentecostal churches. Cephas Omenyo observes that Pentecostalism from the beginning had a distinctive black culture that allowed it to produce a black form of Christianity.[20]

Kalu suggests five additional components that are crucial in the development of the charismatic movements in Nigeria. First is the Hour of Deliverance ministry that operated in Lagos prior to the country's civil war. The second was the charismatic explosion in the Scripture Union in eastern Nigeria between 1967–75. The third is the blossoming of the Hour of Freedom ministry during the Civil War in 1969. Fourth is the growth of the Christian Union Movements in Nigeria's universities, which are discussed more fully in the section below. Finally, there is the Benson Idahosa ministry, which linked the new Christianity with American televangelists.[21]

Christian Unions in Nigerian Universities

In Nigerian universities, a few major groups were established to help bring Christian students together. These were the Student Christian Movement (SCM), Scripture Union (SU), and the Christian Union (CU). They provided the base for the beginning of the charismatic movements. The SCM was founded in 1940 by Dr. Francis Akanu Ibiam, a one-time Eastern Nigerian governor, and Chief Theophilus O. Ejiwumi, one-time secretary to the Western Region, who were introduced to SCM while studying in Britain.[22]

The SCM was established as a mission-oriented organization in British universities in the great missionary era of the nineteenth century. It encouraged students to pledge for missionary work after graduation. When Ibiam returned to Nigeria in 1935, he introduced the SCM to pastors, evangelists, and teachers in the Church of Scotland Mission establishment in Eastern Nigeria where he worked because he was not able to travel to nearby cities with educational institutions.[23]

---

19. Albrecht, *Rites in the Spirit*, 34.
20. Omenyo, *Pentecost Outside Pentecostalism*, 89.
21. Kalu, *African Pentecostalism*, 89.
22. Ojo, "Contextual Significance" 176.
23. Ojo, "Contextual Significance," 176–77.

After Ejiwumi finished his studies at University College, London, on government scholarship, he returned to Yaba Higher College in Lagos by 1940. As a lecturer, he immediately introduced SCM to the students, establishing a branch there.[24] Students who moved from Yaba Higher College started SCM when the University College, Ibadan, was established in 1948 with Ejiwumi as a lecturer.

After 1944, the SCM branch in Ibadan became the center of the SCM in Nigeria. Many British expatriates who were members of the SCM came around to strengthen the group, and in the 1950s SCM groups were formed in the Nigeria colleges of arts and science in the three regions of the country: Ibadan (West), Enugu (East), and Zaria (North). When these colleges became universities in the 1960s, SCM groups continued to grow and flourish. The SCM was instrumental in shaping the lives of the students and the lecturers, and until the mid-1960s the SCM was the only interdenominational Christian student organization in the universities of Ibadan, Ife, Lagos, Nsukka, and Enugu.[25]

The missionaries of the Church Missionary Society introduced the SU to Nigeria in 1844. They emphasized the daily reading of the Bible, especially for children. The expatriate teachers brought the SU into educational institutions. In the early 1960s, SCM began to use the devotional literature of SU to supplement their activities in branches in different universities in Nigeria.

The CU also came from Britain. It was started in 1910 by conservative evangelical members of the SCM at Cambridge University to challenge the liberal theology in the SCM. By 1928, the people who had left the SCM came together to start the Inter-Varsity Christian Fellowship (IVF).[26] This split brought about a demarcation between the SCM with its liberal theological viewpoints and the conservative, evangelical IVF. Their university fellowships adopted the name CU.

As former IVF members were employed as teachers in Nigerian educational institutions, and the people who started Scripture Union in the secondary schools were involved with the universities, CU groups were started in universities as alternatives to the SCM. The SCM emphasized that the gospel could be made relevant to society in terms of political and economic development, while the CU emphasized Bible study and the commitment of individual Christians. The two organizations became prominent influences in what happened to Christian spirituality on the campuses.

The lecturers and students worshipped together in the chapel with the assistance of lecturers in the religious studies department. These were people

24. Ojo, "Contextual Significance," 177.
25. Ojo, "Contextual Significance," 177.
26. Johnson, *Contending for the Faith*, 66–83.

who were ordained in their churches, so they acted as chaplains and patrons. Both fellowships increased in numbers. As Ojo observes, throughout the 1960s, the two groups (SCM and CU) were side by side until the Pentecostal movement arrived.[27]

Ojo, who has done extensive research on Christian fellowships on campuses in Nigeria, says that the influence of the Pentecostal spirit in Nigeria in the 1960s and the 1970s was, to some extent, part of a worldwide movement.[28] Before 1960 the Pentecostal experiences as taught by the Pentecostals were limited to traditional Pentecostal denominations. In 1960 the Rev. Dennis J. Bennett, who was the rector of St. Mark's Church in Los Angeles, openly acknowledged the baptism of the Holy Spirit. After this event, many other non-Pentecostal denominations started acknowledging the experience. This was what some scholars refer to as the *charismatic movement*.[29]

The greater involvement of the young people in Pentecostalism came as a result of the emergence of the *youth culture* in Britain and the USA, which saw a high increase in the student enrollment.[30] In Nigeria, more youths also were interested in going to school, which resulted in the establishment of more universities and other post-secondary institutions in the country and increased the spread of the charismatic revival. The baptism of the Holy Spirit with the evidence of speaking in tongues is one major doctrine among both Pentecostals and charismatic movements.

The first week of January 1970, most of the leaders in the CU in the Ibadan collectively experienced the baptism of the Holy Spirit and speaking in tongues. This incident led to the formation of a Tuesday prayer group for the people who had this Pentecostal experience. They maintained their fellowship with the CU.[31] The group was also involved with vigorous evangelism. From 1970 they started to hold evangelistic retreats in some towns in midwestern, western, and eastern Nigeria, which they called *congresses*. By the middle of 1970, the leaders of the group came together to form an independent and permanent organization: the World Action Team for Christ.[32]

For the next two or three years, the charismatic revival spread from the University of Ibadan to other universities. The universities of Ibadan and Ife became the foremost in this charismatic revival, and some of the graduates of

---

27. Ojo, "Contextual Significance," 178.
28. Ojo, "Charismatic Movement," 114–18.
29. Ojo, "Contextual Significance," 179.
30. Ojo, "Contextual Significance," 178.
31. Ojo, "Contextual Significance," 179.
32. Ojo, "Contextual Significance," 179.

these universities later became the founders and leaders of charismatic organizations. They also pioneered the evangelization of northern Nigeria.[33]

Ojo's account puts the whole influence on the campus fellowships of the CU from Western Nigeria, probably because he is from that part of Nigeria. Kalu, however, insists that the east was not spiritually quiet during the war. He writes that when the schools closed as a result of the war, the new traveling secretary, Bill Roberts, decided to hold Bible classes for students around the SU house in Umuahia. The meeting soon developed into a prayer camp, which led to deep conversion, deliverance, village evangelism, and relief work.[34]

The meeting spurred young people into prayer and evangelistic bands in various villages. Many people had given their lives to Christ, and a lot of healing occurred in many of the hospitals that they visited. Youths began to refuse to take part in the oath taken in the village and refused all forms of idolatry. They became a threat to the status quo. Kalu states, "The young men by their open resistance exposed the compromising ethics of the members of the mainline churches."[35] The ministry of the young men under the leadership of Bill Roberts continued to blossom with more converts from occultism and some Aladura churches. They started the Hour of Freedom.[36]

By the end of the civil war in 1970, the Hour of Freedom members moved to Onitsha, the commercial town of Eastern Nigeria relative to all the villages from the eastern region. They were still members of the SU, but within ten years, revival spread all over Igbo land. A number of the young people who belonged to the Aladura churches joined their parents but soon caused splits within the churches because of the challenge of the use of rituals and symbols in their liturgy.[37]

As mentioned previously, Idahosa, who was converted in the early 1960s under the Assemblies of God in Benin City, built up his ministry through the support of Pa S. G. Elton, a Welsh missionary of the Apostolic Church. This man mentored many young men who were eager to grow. He connected Idahosa with the ministry of Gordon Lindsay and sponsored him to attend Christ for the Nations Bible Institute in Dallas, Texas.[38] Idahosa returned and began a miracle center and television ministry, a Bible school, and a musical group,

---

33. Kalu, Wariboko, and Falola, *Collected Essays*, 2:321; Ojo, "Contextual Significance," 175–92.

34. Kalu, *African Pentecostalism*, 89.

35. Kalu, *African Pentecostalism*, 90.

36. Kalu, *African Pentecostalism*, 90.

37. Kalu, *African Pentecostalism*, 90.

38. He did not complete the course because he claimed that the fire of God was in his bones. Garlock, *Fire in His Bones*, 197.

which all grew rapidly. The leaders of the Hour of Deliverance from Lagos, Elton of the Apostolic Church, Baptist missionary Emma Harris, and a few older charismatic leaders were the source of support for these young people.[39]

By 1973, the federal government of Nigeria established the National Youth Service Corps, which was compulsory for university graduates, and they were posted outside their regions as a way of integrating the country. This posting was a good opportunity to go to different areas of the country, especially the northern part of Nigeria in order to establish various charismatic groups.[40] Because they had the government backing to go to different parts of the country, some of them became traveling secretaries for the Fellowship of Christian Students (FCS).[41]

Some of these vibrant charismatic youths were posted to teach in villages where they continued to preach and pray for people to receive the baptism of the Holy Spirit. A central body was founded in 1973 called Nigerian Christian Corpers Fellowship (NCCF). They also attended Sunday services in the mainline churches, which they considered cold. This led some to begin evangelistic groups for reaching out to people within the church. They were also in the youth groups and the prayer bands.[42] So, Evangelicalism has been strongly influenced by the Pentecostal and charismatic movement in the Nigerian context.

We can safely say that the muddling up of various strands of Christianity in Nigeria has been explained by some African historians like Asamoah Gyadu, Ogbu Kalu, and Matthew Ojo on various levels. Firstly, classical denominations rooted in the 1901 Charles Parham experiences and the 1906 William Seymour Azusa Street Revival in North America gained much prominence in Africa. Then other Pentecostal groups were formed, such as the New Independent Pentecostal Churches (NPCs), transdenominational Pentecostal fellowships like Full Gospel Business Fellowship (FGBMFI), Women Aglow, Intercession for Africa, and charismatic renewal groups of the mainline churches.[43] This is in addition to the blossoming of the Aladura churches (Cherubim and Seraphim Movement, Christ Apostolic Church, and Celestial Church of Christ).[44] The formation of the Evangelical Fellowship in Anglican Communion (EFAC) by John Stott in the Church of England was also important to the Anglican church in Nigeria.

39. Kalu, *African Christianity*, 509, 91–92.
40. Akanya, telephone interview.
41. The Christian Union of the Northern Universities.
42. Akanya, telephone interview.
43. Kalu, *African Christianity*, 341
44. Kalu, *African Christianity*, 339–57

African Evangelicalism, with the influence of the charismatic and Pentecostal brand, has continued to have some major challenges. A few of these I have explored in a previous paper.[45] They include theological challenges, biblical illiteracy and discipleship, corruption and the prosperity gospel, and the challenge of African traditional religion/culture.

Contributions of African Evangelicalism

There are some aspects of success that the African Evangelicals can be proud of, and these could be reflected by different people from various theological persuasions in different lights. However, most African Christians will see these as very important factors that may have contributed to Christianity's success in many parts of Africa.

1. *Emphasis on Prayer*. Unlike the Evangelicalism of the West, the African version has been invigorated with an emphasis on the importance of prayer and the result of prayer as instructed by Jesus in Luke 18:1–8 (that people should pray and not give up) and from Matt 7:7, where Jesus encouraged his disciples to ask, seek, and knock. There are many stories of people who engage in multiple days of prayers and fasting. Many churches in Africa observe nights of prayer. In Nigeria for example, there are many churches that hold Friday night prayer vigils. The Redeemed Christian Church of God camp group on Lagos-Ibadan expressway claims to host over one million people every month. The new area is estimated to seat over three million people. The Catholic, Baptist, and Anglican churches, as well as others, also have regular prayer gatherings where worshippers spend hours in intercession, singing, testimonies, and listening to messages. This prayer emphasis has resulted in some genuine miracles.

2. *Emphasis on Evangelism:* In Africa, Evangelicals believe that they have the duty of preaching the good news of the kingdom of God, and they expect response and conversion. In spite of the persecution in northern Nigeria, conversion to Christianity among Evangelicals is a daily occurrence.

3. *Radical Church Planting*: The need for evangelism is what has also led to radical church planting. For example, the Anglican Church in Nigeria plants more churches every year, and the Redeemed Christian Church

---

45. Oladimeji, "Mentoring," 73–88.

of God has churches in over 190 countries (also consider Living Faith, ECWA, Deeper Life Bible Church, etc.).

4. *Encouragement of Bi-vocationalism*: Some examples are the RCCG (Redeemed Christian Church of God), Winners' Chapel, and the Anglican Church mission in the United States and Canada. Africans have always believed that every area of life should be under the control and lordship of Jesus Christ, and whatever we have should be used to the service of God.

5. *Emphasis on the Supernatural*: Healing, miracles, and deliverance. This makes the Scripture relevant, especially with an African that has been infested with sickness, poverty, and demonic affliction. Many Africans in the West have complained about the dryness of worship among Western-led churches and their anti-spiritual tendencies.

6. *Young People*: Numerical growth of many young people as against many places in the West. Young people are very involved in doing church work. The pastors are encouraged and assessed on their growth, especially numerical growth. "And the Lord added to the church daily such as should be saved" (Acts 2:47 KJV).

7. *Not Much Political Baggage.* In Nigeria, for now, the Evangelicals do not have the type of baggage that they have in the United States. It has been argued that white Evangelicals were major instruments in the election of Donald J. Trump as president of the United States. "He received more than 80 percent of votes cast by white Evangelicals."[46]

Reconstructing African Evangelicalism

It is important for Africa to approach this venture from a point of humility knowing that we cannot be perfect in isolation, hence the need to be willing to continue to learn. Some African leaders believe they cannot be wrong, and if they have "results," it means they are doing the right things and God is blessing them. Here are a few suggestions for reconstructing Evangelicalism to a vibrant, dependable, and effective arm of the Christian faith.

---

46. Gasaway, "Making Evangelicals Great Again?" 293–311.

Global Partnership

Connecting the African church to the Western church in genuine partnership has been a major challenge. This partnership is critical in many ways, but much more from a theological perspective. There has been the popularization of the "three selves" by missiologists since the middle of the twentieth century: self-governing, self-supporting, and self-propagating. Paul Hiebert advocated for the fourth self: self-theologizing.[47] Considering this new self, African churches have tried to reinterpret Scripture and Christian theology within the context of their local culture. The likes of Bolaji Idowu and John Mbiti[48] did a lot of work on this concern from the 1960s into the 1980s. But while that was going on, young Evangelicals like Byang Kato[49] and Tite Titenou[50] cautioned that this could lead to some forms of syncretism. Kato warned in the mid-1970s that Mbiti and Idowu were presenting a Christianity that did not have a clean break from African traditional theology and that this could become dangerous for the future.

There are now various theologies that compete and confuse the average Christian and person in Nigeria. This proliferation has created a relativism in theology, which Hiebert himself feared when he proposed self-theologizing. He suggested what he calls a "metatheology," which Netland defines as "a set of procedures for Christian communities globally that enables local Christian communities to do their theology within their local contexts but in conversation with Christians globally."[51] He affirmed that the Scripture has to be the source of this endeavor. "Just as believers in a local church must test their interpretations of Scripture with their community of believers, so the churches in different cultural and historical contexts must test their theologies with the international community of churches and the church down through the ages. The priesthood of believers must be exercised within a hermeneutical community."[52]

Hiebert feels that there must be a continuous consensus on theological absolutes. But just as it has to involve theologians in various settings, the church in the Western world has its own faults, and Africa, especially Nigerian churches, is not exempt from this problem. Hence, there is the need for

47. Netland, "Introduction," 29.
48. Idowu, *Towards an Indigenous Church*; Mbiti, *African Religions*. While Bolaji Idowu was a Methodist minister from Nigeria in West Africa, John Mbiti was an Anglican Priest from Kenya in East Africa.
49. Kato, *Theological Pitfalls*.
50. Tiénou, *Theological Task*.
51. Netland, "Introduction," 29.
52. Hiebert, *Anthropological Reflections*, 103.

genuine partnership. If the African church is good with prayer and faith in God for their sustenance, how could the church in America learn about this virtue while they enjoy all the safety their society provides?

When we speak of partnership, it is not paternalism. This has been demonstrated in mission partnership, but more so in the denominational splits in the Episcopal Church and United Methodist Church in recent times. The Anglican Church in Nigeria is having a major issue with the Anglican church of North America, which has generated a lot of controversy. While the Anglican church of North America is insisting that the church of Nigeria should relinquish the control of many Nigerian churches in the United States, they have become very reluctant in handing them over, which is now generating a lot of infighting and condemnation from both sides.

Mentoring

There is a mentoring gap. The Deeper Life Bible Church is one of Nigeria's Holiness Evangelical churches. The pastor is over eighty years old. The RCCG has a general overseer who is also over eighty years old. Many other leaders are as old but there is no intentional mentoring. Most of the time mentoring in Nigeria is all about giving money to the "father in the Lord." I have spent some time in my reflection of mentoring the past few years because it is a major challenge in Evangelicalism in Nigeria in general.[53] This is also linked to the lack of accountability among leaders in Africa; it is an African problem. The young ministers seem to be doing their own thing.

Biblical Literacy

It is still concerning to note that apart from a few Evangelicals who are from the older Evangelical churches (ECWA, Baptist, etc.), most of the leaders of Evangelical Christianity do not have the necessary basic theological education. Many of the pastors trained today do not have more than a few weeks of ministry training without any training in biblical interpretation. This is one of the reasons why Nigeria's part in becoming a part of the hermeneutic community has not been feasible.

---

53. Oladimeji, *Fatherless Generation*.

Avoid Politics While Retaining the Prophetic Voice

One challenge that remains is the suspicion of progressive Evangelicalism in America. Progressive Christianity would certainly not be an acceptable brand in Nigeria and many parts of Africa for many decades. There is still the problem of groupthink, which is still very evident in Africa as a collectivist society. However, just like people in the progressive wing such as Jim Wallis, Tony Campolo, and Ron Sider were able to disown and confront Donald Trump on moral and social justice issues, Africa must encourage some sense of autonomy within its ranks.[54]

Conclusion

Evangelicalism in Africa is very different when compared to most parts of the world. It gave Nigeria its foundation in the Christian faith. One priest in the church of Nigeria Anglican communion lamented on the various issues we have mentioned this way:

> The Nigerian Church is quickly losing touch with the authentic, biblical, and historic Christianity and is creating a peculiar Nigerian version, a dangerous trend and brand. . . . This version is loud but lacks content. It misconstrues rattling and noise making for revival. It may be contemporaneous, but it is deviating from the historic Christianity that we received.[55]

This statement is true. However, there are different fruits that have come forth. While we could stand to argue which perspective is the truth, we could decide to pick some of the very important and valuable ingredients, thereby improving our growth and impact globally.

Bibliography

Adogame, Afe U., ed. *Who Is Afraid of the Holy Ghost? Pentecostalism and Globalization in Africa and Beyond.* Trenton, NJ: Africa World, 2011.
Ajaeobi, Joe. Anglican Clergy and Laity Forum, October 3, 2022.
Albrecht, Daniel E. *Rites in the Spirit: A Ritual Approach to Pentecostal/Charismatic Spirituality.* Sheffield, UK: Sheffield Academic, 1999.

---

54. A good example is the Church of Nigeria's issue with women's ministry and acceptance of LGBTQ in the church as worshippers. Some are of a more sympathetic view but cannot publicly affirm their positions.

55. Ajaeobi, Anglican Clergy and Laity Forum.

PART ONE: CHALLENGES

Balcomb Anthony. "Evangelicalism in Africa: What It Is and What It Does." *Missionalia* 44.2 (2016) 117–28.
Bebbington, David. *Evangelicalism in Modern Britain: A History from 1730 to the 1980s*. Grand Rapids: Baker, 1989.
Central Intelligence Agency. "People and Society: Nigeria." The World Factbook. https://www.cia.gov/the-world-factbook/countries/nigeria/#people-and-society.
Garlock, Ruthanne. *Fire in His Bones: The Story of Benson Idahosa*. Plainfield, NJ: Logos International, 1981.
Gasaway, Brantley. "Making Evangelicals Great Again? American Evangelicals in the Age of Trump." *ERT* 43.4 (2019) 293–311.
Hiebert, Paul. *Anthropological Reflections on Missiological Issues*. Grand Rapids: Baker, 1994.
Idowu, Bolaji. *Towards an Indigenous Church*. London: Oxford University Press, 1965.
Johnson, Douglas L. *Contending for the Faith: A History of the Evangelical Movement in the Universities and Colleges*. Leicester, UK: IVP, 1979.
Kalu, Ogbu. *African Christianity: An African Story*. Trenton, NJ: Africa World, 2007.
———. *African Pentecostalism: An Introduction*. Oxford: Oxford University Press, 2008.
Kalu, Wilhelmina, Nimi Wariboko, and Toyin Falola, eds. *The Collected Essays of Ogbu Uke Kalu*. Vol. 2, *Christian Missions in Africa: Mission, Ferment and Trauma*. Trenton, NJ: Africa World, 2010.
Kato, Byang. *Theological Pitfalls in Africa*. Nairobi: Evangel Publishing House, 1975.
Komolafe, Sunday. *The Transformation of African Christianity*. Carlisle, UK: Langham Monographs, 2013.
Mbiti, John. *African Religions and Philosophy*. Garden City, NY: Anchor, 1969.
Netland, Harold. "Introduction: Globalization and Theology Today." In *Globalizing Theology: Belief and Practice in an Era of World Christianity*, edited by Craig Ott and Harold Netland, 14–34. Grand Rapids: Baker Academic, 2006.
Ojo, Matthews. "The Charismatic Movement in Nigeria Today." *IBMR* 19.3 (July 1, 1995) 114–18.
———. "The Contextual Significance of the Charismatic Movements in Independent Nigeria." *Africa* 57.2 (1988) 175–92.
Oladimeji, Babatunde. "Mentoring, Spiritual Formation and African Christianity: The Challenges from the Nigerian Experience." *BET* 7.2 (2020) 73–88.
Oladimeji, Tunde. *The Fatherless Generation—The Challenge of Mentoring in Africa: A Case Study of Leadership Development in Nigerian Christianity*. Saarbrucken, Germany: Lambert Academic, 2015.
Omenyo, Cephas Narh. *Pentecost Outside Pentecostalism: A Study of the Development of Charismatic Renewal in the Mainline Churches in Ghana*. Zoetermeer: Boekencentrum, 2002.
Sweeney, Douglas A. *The American Evangelical Story: A History of the Movement*. Grand Rapids: Baker Academic, 2005.
Tiénou, Tite. *The Theological Task of the Church in Africa*. Nairobi, Kenya: Africa Christian, 1996.
"Who We Are." Association of Evangelicals in Africa, n.d. https://aeafrica.org/about/.
Zurlo, G. A. "Demographics of Global Evangelicalism." In *Evangelicals Around the World: A Global Handbook for the 21st Century*, edited by Brian Stiller and Karen Stiller, 34–47. Nashville, TN: Thomas Nelson, 2015.

Part Two

OPPORTUNITIES

6

The Gospel According to John (Webster)

Toward an Evangelical Evangelical Theology

KEVIN J. VANHOOZER

Introduction

IF THEOLOGY IS THE queen of the sciences, then John Webster was, at the time of his death in 2016, its foremost English prince. A graduate of Cambridge University, he went on to hold professorial chairs at Wycliffe College, Canada, and then at the universities of Oxford, Aberdeen, and finally St. Andrews.

It's probably not accurate to call John a card-carrying Evangelical—at least that wasn't how he would typically introduce himself. However, before he assumed the aforementioned positions, he taught at St. John's College, Durham, an Anglican theological college in the "open Evangelical" tradition, a term used in the United Kingdom to refer to those who hold traditional evangelical doctrines but are perhaps more inclusive than their conservative counterparts when it comes to dialogue partners like Eberhard Jüngel and Karl Barth.

John cared more about theological substance than labels: "He did not pursue independence for its own sake [but] came to be conscious that theology must resist cultural isolations of the wrong sorts, commending its *positum* [positive content] to the world by all the constructive means it can."[1] I suspect

---

1. Davidson, "John Webster," 13.

he would simply shrug his shoulders at the plethora of typologies distinguishing between various kinds of Evangelicals.

It may nevertheless be worth musing on where in the "three worlds" of Evangelicalism Webster belongs.[2] The first or "positive" world is so called because for much of the twentieth century, society had a mostly positive view of Christianity, culminating in *Newsweek* naming 1976 the Year of the Evangelical. This was followed by the "neutral" world (1994–2014), marked by society's growing diffidence toward Christianity, one valid option among others, no more, no less. The third or "negative" world now views Christian morality and politics as a potential threat to freedom and the public good.

For such a negative time as this—of cynicism, hostility, and indifference to Evangelicalism—I propose retrieving the gospel according to John Webster. Evangelicals need to do for Evangelicalism what Webster did for theology, namely, reclaim its true form and content. We begin, then, with a look at his seminal essay, "Theological Theology." We then examine what Webster has to say about the "gospel" and investigate how he uses the term "evangelical." The aim of the exercise is not to replicate Webster's own position, but to appropriate his approach and use his insights as a stimulus for articulating and embodying a truly *evangelical* Evangelicalism.

"Theological Theology": Cleansing the Ivory Temple of the Doctrine-changers

Webster gave his inaugural lecture, "Theological Theology," upon becoming Lady Margaret Professor of Divinity at the University of Oxford in 1997. It's worth recalling that what Webster was reacting to back then, call it non-theological theology, bears certain similarities to our present situation, which we might describe, provocatively, as non-evangelical Evangelicalism.

On the Oxfordian Captivity of the Queen

More specifically, Webster rebutted what he saw as a certain Babylonian captivity, not of the church but of the discipline of theology itself—a captivity to Berlin and Oxford, which is to say, the institution of modern academia. As a student, Webster had been taught that theology depended on other disciplines, like literary theory or epistemology, to make intelligible truth claims. Having to conform to standards of rationality, theology was not free to be itself. The queen of the sciences was imprisoned in an ivory tower.

2. See Renn, "Three Worlds of Evangelicalism."

Webster could have called his inaugural lecture, "The Scandal of the Theological Mind." The scandal, for Webster, was twofold: first, theologians were not viewing their minds theologically, namely, as created intellects that were fallen, requiring regeneration. Second, theology was not being taken seriously in modern Western universities but was "most often treated with a benign indifference."[3] Modern theology had lost its saltiness; it had "internalized the models of enquiry which [had] become normative in modern academic institutions."[4] It had bowed to the assumption that intellectual inquiry "ought to be as unaffected by the specificities of culture, personality, or political and religious conviction as is the functioning of the bodily organs."[5] In short, modern theology had lost its home-field advantage and was always playing away games, adhering to general standards of acceptability and respectability.

Webster trains his critical guns not only on the prevailing academic culture, however, but also on "a certain failure of theological nerve."[6] He continues, "The intellectual disarray of modern Christian theology owes as much to its loss of confidence in its own habits of mind as it does to the enmity sometimes shown by its cultural context."[7] Consequently, it has become difficult for biblical exegetes, historians, and theologians "to state with any clarity what is specifically *theological* about their enquiries."[8] Where Webster says *theological*, we can also read *evangelical*. For it has become increasingly difficult for exegetes, pastors, and theologians to say what is specifically evangelical about their commentaries, sermons, and doctrines. Where modern theology was assimilated to other discourses in the academy, so American Evangelicalism has been assimilated to broader trends in culture and politics.

The Proper Object of Theology: God and All Things in Relation to God

Webster does not want theology to have a seat at the university table if that means politely observing a single set of standards for dinner conversation; we do not come to know God we as do other objects of study. The proper object of theology is "the eschatological self-presence of God in Jesus Christ through

---

3. Webster, "Theological Theology," 12.
4. Webster, "Theological Theology," 12.
5. Webster, "Theological Theology," 14.
6. Webster, "Theological Theology," 17.
7. Webster, "Theological Theology," 17.
8. Webster, "Theological Theology," 22.

the power of the Holy Spirit."⁹ Focusing for too long on anything else is a distraction. Theologians should have a confident and cheerful sense "of the importance of non-conformity."¹⁰ The university table should, ideally, be a place of energetic "conversations about differing visions of human life and thought," and the theologian should be the articulate and competent voice of Christian faith and practice.¹¹

In retrospect, Webster was not satisfied with his lecture, believing he was still talking too much about human practices and not enough about God. He therefore returned to the topic in an essay asking, "What makes theology theological?"¹² The answer: a resolute focus on the triune God and everything else in relation to God. This is possible only because God communicates to creatures a share in his knowledge: revelation is an invitation to rational creatures to enjoy "intelligent fellowship" with God.¹³ Worship and everyday devotion to God are the fitting practical expressions of fellowship with God. Whether we work or play, eat or drink, our attention should be fixed in wonder, love, and praise on God who is the cause and end of all things, not on the things of which God is the cause. This settled focus is, for Webster, what makes theology theological.

Against Non-theological Theology

In a preliminary sketch for the proposed dogmatic theology he was never able to write, Webster returned again to the theme of his inaugural lecture, bemoaning the prevailing tendency to let *non-theological* fields of inquiry furnish theology with its "tools of analysis . . . patterns of thought . . . subject matter, or procedures."¹⁴ A student once asked Webster, "How do we engage conversations in academia as faithful Evangelicals?" Webster responded by cautioning the student against the ever-present temptation to seek higher social status, including academic status. The siren call of intellectual respectability leads some Evangelicals to conform to mainstream academic trends, methods, and institutions in order to be accepted. Webster encouraged his listeners to participate in the guild, but also to maintain a critical distance rather than selling their souls out of Faustian desperation.

---

9. Webster, "Theological Theology," 26.
10. Webster, "Theological Theology," 28.
11. Webster, "Theological Theology," 27.
12. Webster, "What Makes Theology Theological?," 213–24.
13. Webster, "What Makes Theology Theological?," 217.
14. Cited in Nelson, "Epilogue," 301.

It is tempting even for Christian theologians, like their ancient Israelite forebears, to want to be like the other nations—to be ruled not by a king, but by the same intellectual standards as other disciplines. Webster's prophetic "Thou art the discipline!" is a call for theologians (and, indirectly, Evangelicals) to have confidence in their own God-given resources—their own distinctly Christian texts, traditions, and practices.

Webster on the Gospel: The Gift of Fellowship with God in Christ

In this second section, I examine Webster's varied description of the gospel, roughly in chronological fashion, over the last twenty years of his life.

Theology's Form: "Rational Speech about the Christian Gospel"

In his 1995 Wycliffe College inaugural address, "Reading Theology," Webster ties theology to the gospel in no uncertain terms: "Theology serves the Word of God by assisting the Church to remain faithful to the gospel as it is manifest in Holy Scripture."[15] Moreover, theology serves the *church* by clarifying its identity in relation to the gospel, and by preserving its identity, not least in distinguishing what belongs to the gospel from what is merely a cultural accretion. Webster cannot conceive of Christian theology apart from the gospel because it just is "rational speech about the Christian gospel."[16] The centrality of the gospel is apparent in my favorite Webster definition of Christian theology: "that delightful activity in which the church praises God by ordering its thinking toward the gospel of Christ."[17] Formally, then, the gospel is that to which the church orders its thinking and living. It is "normatively set forth in Holy Scripture . . . that collection of writings generated by and appointed to serve the self-communication of God."[18]

Theology's Material Content: "Indicative of Reconciliation through the Son"

As to the material content of the gospel, it is the announcement "that in and as the man Jesus Christ . . . God creates, reconciles, and perfects all things."[19]

---

15. Webster, "Reading Theology," 56.
16. Webster, "Introduction," in *Word and Church*, 3.
17. Webster, "Introduction," in *Word and Church*, 1.
18. Webster, "Confession and Confessions," 75.
19. Webster, "Introduction," in *Word and Church*, 4.

The gospel is the announcement that, in Christ, humanity has received the gift of fellowship with God. It is "the joyful and awed affirmation that the Word became flesh,"[20] an "astonished indication" of what God has done in Christ, an "indicative of reconciliation through the Son."[21] With its indicative statements, theology points or witnesses "to the order of reality declared in the gospel."[22] The gospel is the good news that, in Christ, we are new creatures, and that the Christian life is best described in terms of election, creation, justification, sanctification, and glorification.

Theology's Scope: "There Is Nothing that the Gospel Does Not Explicate"

Although Webster kept track of academic trends and cultural fads, his is no seeker-sensitive theology. "Context" for Webster is simply the occasion for articulating the gospel in a particular place and time: "This—the progress of the gospel through the occasions of human life—is theology's context, which is properly spiritual and therefore properly a matter for theological description."[23] The history of the church is simply a series of attempts to articulate the gospel in varying contexts. Moreover, "To reckon with the Christian gospel was, for Webster, to be interested in all kinds of things, for there was no sphere of reality not encompassed by that gospel's address."[24] Fred Sanders makes the same point in a 2016 tribute to Webster: "There is nothing that the gospel does not explicate."[25] The gospel may not say everything that needs to be said, but in saying what is in Christ, it casts light on all things everywhere.

In his later work, Webster lays greater and greater emphasis on the presupposition of the gospel: "the presence of the perfect God."[26] The God who is with us is the God who is full of himself, as it were—majesty without measure. The good news is that God's perfect life "includes the willing and execution of a movement of love in which he glorifies himself by bringing into being a creature for himself . . . and ensuring that it will attain its own perfection."[27] The gospel is eschatological because it is not this-worldly: the God who is with us is unattainable through history, culture, or even peace and justice

---

20. Webster, "Incarnation," 132.
21. Nimmo, "Ethics," 288.
22. Webster, "Introduction," in *Word and Church*, 4.
23. Webster, "Introduction," in *Word and Church*, 5.
24. Davidson, "John Webster," 13.
25. Sanders, "John Webster," para. 20.
26. Webster, "Introduction," in *Confessing God*, 1.
27. Webster, "Introduction," in *Confessing God*, 2.

activism. For this reason, the gospel cannot be coerced, only confessed: "To confess is to cry out in acknowledgement of the sheer gratuity of what the gospel declares."[28] A confessional formula, like a statement of faith, is "a *public and binding indication of the gospel.*"[29] Yet Webster's caution against weaponizing statements of faith is also noteworthy: "A creed is not a programme, a platform, a manifesto to mobilize our forces. It is an amazed cry of witness: 'Behold, the Lamb of God.' . . . Confession is attestation, not self-assertion."[30] A creed is "an aspect of the church's exegetical fellowship, of learning alongside the saints and doctors and martyrs how to give ear to the gospel."[31]

The gospel according to John Webster is not only gracious and capacious, but also solicitous: "The consolation which the gospel brings is its announcement that the world really is a place where God in Christ reigns with the unleashed power of the Holy Spirit."[32] To recover this theological understanding of the gospel is no easy task in a "negative" world. In order to appreciate what Webster has in mind by "gospel," then, we must make every possible effort to saturate our imaginations in its astonished indications. For "gospel" refers first and foremost to what God has said and done in Christ. "Evangelical" in its truest, most theological sense, means corresponding to the gospel: thinking God's thoughts after him and, more importantly, responding to every situation in a manner that corresponds to the new reality that is in Christ. To be a people of the gospel is to speak, think, hope, and act "in accordance with the way in which the Christian gospel declares the world to be."[33] To be truly evangelical is to get real.

Webster's Use of the Term "Evangelical": Corresponding to the Gospel

We turn now to examine Webster's use of the term "evangelical." We will look at what it means and the kinds of things it qualifies, in particular, theology, freedom, and the church.

---

28. Webster, "Confession and Confessions," 71.
29. Webster, "Confession and Confessions," 74 (emphasis original).
30. Webster, "Confession and Confessions," 74.
31. Webster, "Confession and Confessions," 76.
32. Webster, "Confession and Confessions," 79.
33. Webster, "Hope," 195.

"Evangelical" Theology

Sadly, we will never know what Webster's multi-volume dogmatics would have been like, though we do have some hints. In the proposal he submitted to the publishers (Baker Academic), he described the project as "evangelical" theology, but in "the German sense of *evangelisch* rather than the more restricted North American sense of a particular blend of modern Protestant developments."[34] He planned to focus less on cultural trends and contextual factors than on descriptions of theology's proper subject matter, the processions and missions of the triune God, and to do so largely by expositing Scripture.[35] The priority of biblical exegesis is evident in his most succinct definition of "evangelical" that I have to date been able to find: "governed by the gospel of Christ."[36]

To say "evangelical" is, for Webster, to describe the divine initiative that is the ground for human salvation and human freedom alike. Evangelical thinking means engaging "with the gospel of God's covenant-restoring mercy of which the Son's presence and mission are the enactments and of which the Spirit is the communicative presence."[37]

I interviewed John in 2011 as part of a public event at Wheaton College. I asked him how important he thought the qualifier "evangelical" was to his work, and what work the term does when it qualifies theology. He replied that he was not "custodial" about the term, but that it should not be infinitely elastic either. Primarily, it means gospel-centered; secondarily, it connects one to particular aspects of the Christian tradition (here both my memory and my notes fail me, as I am not sure which aspects he had in mind). What I do remember is his insistence that we are entrusted with God's gospel and must not stray from it and, if we do stray, that we are no longer in the business of theology.

"Evangelical" Freedom

In 2003 Webster weighed in on the issue of homosexuality with an essay entitled "Evangelical Freedom."[38] His negative point was that freedom as

---

34. Cited in Nelson, "Epilogue," 300.

35. Michael Reeves rightly notes that the attempt to define Evangelicalism sociologically or descriptively rather than biblically and theologically "is precisely the problem at the heart of the evangelical identity crisis today." *Gospel People*, 126.

36. Webster, "What's Evangelical?," 179.

37. Webster, "What's Evangelical?," 184.

38. Webster, "Evangelical Freedom," 215–26.

self-determination is a modern cultural convention. The problem with the modern conception is that human and divine freedom seem to be on a collision course. This is a disordered concept of freedom: "to think of the world as the kind of place where human freedom can only be maintained if we think of that freedom as self-governance is to think of the world untruthfully."[39] By way of positive response, Webster described the freedom announced in the gospel.

Evangelical dogmatics and ethics alike order their thinking to the gospel as an *indicative* claim to truth. An evangelical dogmatics expounds on the gospel's announcement of God's freedom to be with and for us. An evangelical ethics orders its thinking toward the gospel as an *imperative*, a call to action, and a summons to freedom in Christ.[40] An evangelical theology of freedom avoids polarizing human and divine freedom, insisting instead that humans discover true freedom only in fellowship with, and obedience to, God the Father. This is the kind of freedom for which we are set free in Christ. True human freedom is "the capacity to realize what one is . . . to be what I have been made to be."[41]

"Evangelical" Ecclesiology

I conclude my survey of Webster's use of the term "evangelical" with his 2004 essay "On Evangelical Ecclesiology."[42] It's fitting that we end with Webster's understanding of the church, first, because Evangelicalism is typically viewed as a branch of the church; second, because ecclesiology is a soft spot in evangelical theology, and arguably at the root of the present confusion about this diffuse movement. Webster was an ecclesial theologian, not because he thought theology was something the church had to do but, rather, because he viewed the church as itself thoroughly theological: a work of God that brings sinners into the society of God. The theological nature of the church comes to the fore in a later essay, in which Webster cites Bonhoeffer approvingly: "the concept of church is conceivable only in the sphere of reality established by God."[43]

Interestingly enough, it was only when Webster reflected on the church's turn to community practices (think Hauerwas) and pragmatism (think North

39. Webster, "Evangelical Freedom," 219.
40. Webster, "Evangelical Freedom," 220.
41. Webster, "Evangelical Freedom," 223–24.
42. Webster, "On Evangelical Ecclesiology," 153–93 (reprinted in *Community of the Word*, 75–113. Citations come from this latter source).
43. Cited in Webster, "In the Society of God," 222.

America) that he was awakened from his undogmatic ecclesial slumber.[44] The tendency to see the church as a social project and to treat ecclesiology as "first theology" are but two of the many ways in which Webster considered contemporary theology "disordered." They are symptoms that the church has been in her own head for far too long, preoccupied with her identity and the way she appears to the outside world. We need to get out of our own heads in order to remember that the church's true head is Jesus Christ.

Webster would probably see most contemporary attempts to "do" church or "fix" the church as fundamentally disordered. Over the past few decades, we have witnessed a plethora of such experiments: seeker-sensitivity training, slow church, deep church, megachurch, metachurch (digital ministry), missional church, simple church, celebrity church, ancient-future church, emerging church, and so on. We have followed programs, imitated best practices, and adopted strategies from the business world, entertainment industry, leadership studies, and the sports field, all in the somewhat desperate pursuit of church growth and ministry success. Like nature, ecclesiology abhors a vacuum, and in the absence of a robust theological account of the church's nature and mission, human programs and practices have rushed in to fill the void. Their name is Legion.

Webster's verdict is pointed: "It is not the task of dogmatics to underwrite the practices of the church but to submit them to judgment. . . . And the criterion by which it makes its judgment is . . . the gospel announced in Holy Scripture."[45] An evangelical ecclesiology is one that "is evoked, governed, and judged by the gospel."[46] According to Webster's understanding of the gospel, an evangelical church is not simply a group of people who gather together because they share a common morality or politics. Rather, a church that corresponds to the gospel is a people that God gathers to himself to form a holy nation. The only politics that matters is that which corresponds to our citizenship of the gospel (Phil 3:20).

Yes, the church is visible—some might say *too* visible, warts and all—yet Webster reminds us that the church "is not constituted by human intentions, activities and institutional or structural forms, but by the action of the triune God."[47] What gathers the people of God and makes for an evangelical church is not the youth program, or the fabulous preaching, or the wonderful music, only the gospel ministry of Word and Spirit, nothing more, nothing less. Webster is therefore most interested in the *invisible* or theological character of the

---

44. See Webster, "Ecclesiocentrism."
45. Webster, "Self-Organizing Power of the Gospel," 194.
46. Webster, "Self-Organizing Power of the Gospel," 191.
47. Webster, "Self-Organizing Power of the Gospel," 195.

church's visible life. To give a thick description of the church, we need more than sociology. We need the resources of Trinitarian theology.[48]

The existence of the church—the new society ordered in Christ—is an implication of the gospel, the result of God's determination to be with and for human creatures. Why is there church rather than nothing? Because God was in Christ, reconciling the world to himself (2 Cor 5:19). God's determination to fellowship with sinners generates a unique social space. Thanks to the work of the Holy Spirit, "The gospel of reconciliation becomes visible in creaturely relations and actions."[49] The church is made up not of *nice* people, but *new* people. This is evangelical ecclesiology: "The church is because God is and acts *thus* . . . the gospel precedes and the church follows."[50] We may choose which local church to attend, but a church only exists because God has first chosen to create it. To confess our belief in the communion of saints is to acknowledge the eschatological work of the Holy Spirit. The church is a fellowship of saints in the society of God.[51] The bond that unites us goes deeper than local church or denominational membership. It is an evangelical unity—gospel generated and governed—in which we are blessed "with every spiritual blessing in the heavenly places" (Eph 1:3).

To describe the visible church as "evangelical," then, is to say that "*it is what men and women do because of the gospel.*"[52] What exactly are they, or should they, be doing? In a word: bearing witness to what the triune God has done, attesting to the reality of a new social order in Christ in which the new wine of reconciliation bursts the old wineskins of ethnic and social hostility. The church "simply *points*"[53]—in word, sacrament, and common life alike. A truly evangelical ecclesiology views the church first and foremost as an astonished indication of the truth and reality of the gospel.

"Evangelical" Evangelicalism: Doctrine, Life, and Church as Astonished Indications of the Gospel

I trust we now have a better sense of what Webster means by "evangelical," and thus of what it would mean to pursue an *evangelical* Evangelicalism. The gospel, according to John Webster, is what generates, guides, governs, and

---

48. See also Mangina, "Church," and my "Ecclesiology as a Dogmatic Discipline."
49. Webster, "Church and the Perfection of God," 76.
50. Webster, "Church and the Perfection of God," 76.
51. Webster, "Church and the Perfection of God," 90.
52. Webster, "Visible Attests the Invisible," 101 (my emphasis).
53. Webster, "Visible Attests the Invisible," 106 (emphasis original).

judges everything that attempts to pass as "evangelical." It is a severe grace—grace, because it concerns the unmerited divine decision to be with and for us; severe, because it summons would-be Evangelicals to see, think, do, and judge in accordance with the reality the gospel announces: "Theology serves the Word of God by assisting the church to remain alert to the challenge of the gospel as it is manifest in Holy Scripture."[54]

Is this sheer idealism or does it make a difference on the ground, in the way Evangelicals walk the sawdust trail? At the very least, the idea of *evangelical* Evangelicalism clarifies what ails us: a failure to take seriously the theological nature of the term and the movement.

Three Sub-evangelical Tendencies in Contemporary Evangelicalism

Let me here identify three tendencies that have tarnished the reputation of Evangelicals and distorted the true meaning of the term "evangelical." The common factor is a flirtation, if not outright affiliation, with a *different* gospel. What concerned Paul about the first-century church at Corinth has come to pass in twenty-first-century North America: "As the serpent deceived Eve by his cunning, your thoughts will be led astray from a sincere and pure devotion to Christ. For if . . . you accept a different gospel from the one you accepted, you submit to it readily enough" (2 Cor 11:3–4 ESV).

(1) *A "negative" (i.e., reactionary) theology.* For much of the twentieth century, evangelical theology has been reactionary, fearful, and on the defensive. The bane of evangelical existence, as Donald Bloesch has noted, is its tendency to major on the minors—to wage internecine warfare over non-Nicene theology. This has damaged the unity of the church and the integrity of our witness. For as 1 John 4:18 does *not* say: perfect fear casts out love.

(2) *An only human/cultural freedom.* Sadly, many self-confessed, churchgoing Evangelicals assert and employ their individual freedom in sub-evangelical ways that do not correspond to their newness in Christ. David Wells has chronicled the ways in which North American Evangelicals have adopted cultural practices that tacitly proclaim a different gospel. They may affirm *sola scriptura*, but they live as if they actually believed in *sola cultura*.[55]

(3) *An onerous exchange: gospel vs. American citizenship.* I call the third sub-evangelical distortion the onerous exchange, that all-too-obvious transfer of political allegiance from their holy nation—the church, the city of God (Exod 19:6; 1 Pet 2:9)—to some earthly nation. It is like selling one's birthright,

---

54. Webster, "Reading Theology," 59.
55. Wells, *Courage to Be Protestant*, 7.

gospel citizenship, for a bowl of red (MAGA?) stew or for the sexy look of global cosmopolitanism. The use of the faith for the sake of party politics and earthly ideologies is a distortion of both the biblical gospel and Jesus's own teaching.[56]

Righting the Good Ship Evangelical with the Positum of the Gospel

Emboldened by Webster, I conclude with three theses on how to infuse the term *evangelical*, and the movement that wears the identifying label, with positive content, and a positive charge, in the midst of a "negative" world.

(1) An *evangelical* evangelical theology should bear positive witness, despite the surrounding negative world. The essence of evangelical evangelical theology has less to do with a reactionary circling of the doctrinal wagons than it does with articulating the doctrinal essentials. These stem from a whole series of "astonished" indications that, together, unpack the length, breadth, height, and depth of God's reconciling act in Christ.

(2) An *evangelical* evangelical freedom will freely and joyfully appropriate and inhabit these indicatives of the gospel, thanks in large part to a robust eschatological imagination. The evangelical imperatives that follow from the evangelical indicatives ultimately amount simply to this: become what you already are in Christ.

(3) An *evangelical* evangelical church testifies to *sola scriptura* not merely with formal affirmations about biblical authority or scholarly societies whose membership requires belief in inerrancy, important though they may be, but, rather, by adopting the gospel alone as her social imaginary. After all, to think about the evangelical church evangelically is to view the church as the hands and feet of the mind of Christ, a bodily function of the society of Jesus. This society—the people of God, the body of Christ, the fellowship of the Spirit—must operate with a social imaginary ruled by the biblical gospel alone. When it does, the visible church attests the gospel of God. The church is therefore as essential to evangelical theology as evangelical theology is to the church: evangelical theology without the church is a disembodied abstraction; the church without evangelical theology is an absent-minded busybody.

Conclusion

In sum: an *evangelical* Evangelicalism generates and governs doctrine, freedom, and church such that they become forms—propositional, practical, and

---

56. See further Campbell, *Jesus v. Evangelicals*.

doxological—of astonished and joyful indications of the gospel, theoretical and practical pointers to the good news that the kingdom of God has indeed come near. An *evangelical* Evangelicalism is proof that a new humanity—being "in Christ" with others through the Holy Spirit—is ours even now, by grace through faith.[57] May *this* tribe increase!

Bibliography

Campbell, Constantine. *Jesus v. Evangelicals: A Biblical Critique of a Wayward Movement*. Grand Rapids: Zondervan, 2023.

Davidson, Ivor J. "John Webster (1955–2016)." In *A Companion to the Theology of John Webster*, edited by Michael Allen and R. David Nelson, 1–18. Grand Rapids: Eerdmans, 2021.

———. "Salvation." In *A Companion to the Theology of John Webster*, edited by Michael Allen and R. David Nelson, 223–44. Grand Rapids: Eerdmans, 2021.

Mangina, Joseph L. "The Church." In *A Companion to the Theology of John Webster*, edited by Michael Allen and R. David Nelson, 245–63. Grand Rapids: Eerdmans, 2021.

Nelson, David R. "Epilogue: Courses Charted but Not Taken." In *A Companion to the Theology of John Webster*, edited by Michael Allen and R. David Nelson, 297–314. Grand Rapids: Eerdmans, 2021.

Nimmo, Paul T. "Ethics." In *A Companion to the Theology of John Webster*, edited by Michael Allen and R. David Nelson, 280–96. Grand Rapids: Eerdmans, 2021.

Reeves, Michael. *Gospel People: A Call for Evangelical Integrity*. Wheaton, IL: Crossway, 2022.

Renn, Aaron M. "The Three Worlds of Evangelicalism." *First Things*, February 2022. https://www.firstthings.com/article/2022/02/the-three-worlds-of-Evangelicalism.

Sanders, Fred. "John Webster, 1955–2016: 'There Is Nothing that the Gospel Does Not Explicate.'" *The Scriptorium Daily*, May 26, 2016. https://scriptoriumdaily.com/john-webster-1955-2016-there-is-nothing-that-the-gospel-does-not-explicate/.

Vanhoozer, Kevin J. "Ecclesiology as a Dogmatic Discipline." In *T&T Clark Handbook of Ecclesiology*, edited by Kimlyn Bender and D. Stephen Long, 293–310. London: T&T Clark, 2020.

———. "Evangelicalism and the Church: The Company of the Gospel." In *The Futures of Evangelicalism: Issues and Prospects*, edited by Craig Bartholomew, Robin Parry, and Andrew West, 40–99. Leicester, UK: InterVarsity, 2003.

Webster, John. "The Church and the Perfection of God." In *The Community of the Word: Toward an Evangelical Ecclesiology*, edited by Mark Husbands and Daniel J. Treier, 75–95. Downers Grove, IL: IVP Academic, 2005.

———. "Confession and Confessions." In *Confessing God: Essays in Christian Dogmatics II*, 69–83. London: Bloomsbury T&T Clark, 2005.

———. "Ecclesiocentrism: A Review of *Hauerwas: A (Very) Critical Introduction*." *First Things*, October 2014. https://www.firstthings.com/article/2014/10/ecclesiocentrism.

———. "Evangelical Freedom." In *Confessing God: Essays in Christian Dogmatics II*, 215–26. London: Bloomsbury T&T Clark, 2005.

---

57. See further my "Evangelicalism and the Church."

———. "Hope." In *Confessing God: Essays in Christian Dogmatics II*, 195–214. London: Bloomsbury T&T Clark, 2005.

———. "'In the Society of God': Some Principles of Ecclesiology." In *Perspectives on Ecclesiology and Ethnography*, edited by Pete Ward, 200–22. Grand Rapids: Eerdmans, 2012.

———. "Incarnation." In *Word and Church: Essays in Christian Dogmatics*, 113–50. London: Bloomsbury T&T Clark, 2001.

———. "Introduction." In *Confessing God: Essays in Christian Dogmatics II*, 1–8. London: Bloomsbury T&T Clark, 2005.

———. "Introduction." In *Word and Church: Essays in Christian Dogmatics*, 1–6. London: Bloomsbury T&T Clark, 2001.

———. "On Evangelical Ecclesiology." In *The Community of the Word: Toward an Evangelical Ecclesiology*, edited by Mark Husbands and Daniel J. Treier, 75–113. Downers Grove, IL: IVP Academic, 2005.

———. "Reading Theology." *Toronto Journal of Theology* 13.1 (1997) 53–63.

———. "The Self-organizing Power of the Gospel of Christ: Episcopacy and Community Formation." In *Word and Church: Essays in Christian Dogmatics*, 191–210. Edinburgh: T&T Clark, 2001.

———. "Theological Theology." In *Confessing God: Essays in Christian Dogmatics II*, 11–31. London: Bloomsbury T&T Clark, 2005.

———. "The Visible Attests the Invisible." In *The Community of the Word: Toward an Evangelical Ecclesiology*, edited by Mark Husbands and Daniel J. Treier, 96–113. Downers Grove, IL: IVP Academic, 2005.

———. "What Makes Theology Theological?" In *God without Measure*, vol. 1, *God and the Works of God*, 213–24. London: Bloomsbury T&T Clark, 2016.

———. "What's Evangelical about Evangelical Soteriology?" In *What Does It Mean to Be Saved? Expanding Evangelical Horizons of Salvation*, edited by John G. Stackhouse, 179–84. Grand Rapids: Baker Academic, 2002.

Wells, David F. *The Courage to Be Protestant: Reformation Faith in Today's World*. Grand Rapids: Eerdmans, 2017.

7

Seeing the World through Bavinckian Eyes

GAYLE DOORNBOS

Introduction

EVEN FOR THOSE OUTSIDE of the evangelical ecosphere, it is hard to deny that the landscape of American ecclesial life is shifting. While it has always been complex and marred, over the last decade those living in it have increasingly experienced the reality of leaders and churches flailing and falling under narcissistic leaders, abuse scandals becoming shockingly regular, deep strife and rifts emerging as a result of the presence of civil religion (on both the right and the left), and denominations and individual churches rending themselves apart over matters related to human sexuality. The result for those of us who live in the ecclesial land of American Christianity is that we often feel like wanderers in terrain that used to seem familiar. There are fault lines and polarization; the landscape contains fences where we used to find tables and shared meals. We notice darkness and scorched patches, marking out sadness and pain we never knew was there. We find holes and escape hatches where we used to find friends. We notice growing fissures in the buildings that once stood as seemingly impenetrable fortresses. As our landscape shifts, frays, and is rearranged, our sense of what should be or how we should navigate this terrain is becoming less clear.[1]

---

1. This is not to claim that the church in America is in complete ruins, nor is it to call for the formation of a "Back to Egypt Committee" to resurrect a period now past. The previous

Some anthropologists, social theorists, and theologians have begun to label our current context a "liminal space," or what Mark Sayers describes in his new book, *A Non-Anxious Presence*, a "grey space."[2] The concept of liminality derived from anthropology originally described traditional rites of passage, usually from childhood to adulthood. In this context, liminality described the in-between phase for adolescents as children were separated from their old identity and transitioned to adulthood. However, applied more broadly, liminal spaces/times are being employed to describe social or cultural contexts marked by significant shifts and transitions. In themselves, liminal spaces are not inherently bad. However, they can spark fear, uncertainty, and anxiety individually and collectively, especially when they are the result of the collapse or change of the social bulwarks that used to provide some sense of stability, meaning, and identity.[3] This is especially true when there seems to be no clear picture of what's next.

One does not need to dig too deep to see that the shifts in our current ecclesial and social life, often arising out of the deeper cultural shifts so aptly described by Charles Taylor in his work *A Secular Age*, have created a liminal space marked by anxiety. Some scholars have begun to diagnose American society itself as chronically anxious, producing a cultural context in which reactivity, blame displacement, a quick-fix mentality, herding, and a lack of well-differentiated leadership are the norm.[4] As one cultural commentator, Susan Beaumont, suggests, this chronic anxiety fuels political, social, and ecclesial action bringing about fissures, renewed tribalism, and a willingness to follow anyone who promises stability (no matter how empty the promise may be).[5]

This raises the question, what does it look like to lead now, and what is required to navigate this landscape? How do pastor theologians engage the questions that have arisen in our current landscape, questions that, while

---

ecclesial landscape was not a lush forest nor the garden of Eden; it already contained many of the fissures, abuses, and challenges that have been coming into full and horrific bloom. However, the shifts within our common ecclesial landscape have deeply impacted pastors. Their journeys have often come with pain, exhaustion, burnout, and deep grief.

2. Sayers, *Non-Anxious Presence*, 19–21.

3. The term "liminal space" originates from Arnold van Gennop, who used the word to describe transition rites that he observed in various cultures. He described these rites as containing three phases: separation (from old identity), liminality (in-between), and incorporation into new group identity.

4. See, for example, Friedman, *Failure of Nerve*, 51–94. Friedman applies Bowen's family systems theory to the work of cultural analysis in his book and diagnoses contemporary culture as chronically anxious. His book is deeply insightful diagnostically, even if it can be read to support a variety of positions on how to engage contemporary culture.

5. Beaumont, *How to Lead*, 113.

novel in the history of the church, are nonetheless being asked from social and ecclesial locations?

Bavinck: A Guide for a Liminal Age

There are many good ways to approach this question, but one reason why the idea of liminality is helpful is that in its anthropological origins, it highlights that one of the things we need in liminal spaces are guides who lead the way. In traditional rites of passage, guides serve to aid the process of transition, pointing the way and helping the child inhabit the new unfamiliar space. They provide a tether to what was and what will be. As guides were a vital aspect within traditional rites of passage, so too good guides are imperative within our current context. We need guides to point the way and to form our imaginations to engage creatively and well.

While there are many such guides, this chapter offers Herman Bavinck (1854–1921), a Dutch theologian from the turn of the twentieth century, as one such guide. Standing alongside other guides, Bavinck's specific contribution is a theological one. Namely, he is a guide that can form our theological imaginations to engage and interact with our liminal context in grounded yet dynamic and nonanxious ways. While Bavinck's theological vision is not a panacea for every ecclesial or cultural ill, he can serve as a guide to help us chart our way as we wander in lands that used to seem familiar. Part of the reason Bavinck is a good guide is because of his own social-ecclesial location. He too lived through a time of significant upheaval and societal change.

Contrary to common assumptions, the nineteenth century was not a bygone era in which stability reigned and the church—at least in the West— experienced some form of a golden age. The nineteenth century was a time of radical change across Europe. In the Netherlands, modernization began to take hold and leave its mark on "every square inch" of Dutch society in the second half of the nineteenth century. As summarized by historian Arie L. Molendijk, modernity was a far-reaching movement defined by: (1) capitalist industrialization, (2) political modernization (in the formation of the modern state with political parties), (3) the pluralization of society and a growing separation of state and society, (4) the development of individualistic lifestyles, and (5) "the privatization of religion and a concomitant deinstitutionalization of religion."[6] Societal shifts, ecclesial fractures, religious decline, and new waves of wealth and opportunities alongside extreme poverty marked life in the Netherlands

---

6. Molendijk, *Protestant Theology*, 3.

throughout the nineteenth century.[7] By the turn of the twentieth century, those living in the Netherlands were also wandering in lands that used to look familiar. This was the world into which Bavinck was born and the context in which he developed his theology. Neo-Calvinism, the complex and somewhat variegated movement started by Bavinck and Abraham Kuyper, was developed in response to the aforementioned shifts. Neo-Calvinism found in Calvinism a creation-wide vision that included every aspect of life; this cultural and ecclesial engagement was grounded in a deep and rich theological vision.[8]

In this chapter, it is not possible to explore the full scope of Bavinck's theology, but there are three texts spanning across twenty-five years that capture Bavinck's theological vision and the way it informs his engagement within a shifting world: (1) a sermon on 1 John 5:4 from 1901, (2) "The Catholicity of Christianity" (1888), and (3) "Christianity" (1912).

THE WORLD-CONQUERING POWER OF FAITH

While Bavinck preached often, only one sermon exists in manuscript form: Bavinck's sermon on a text he preached on many times, 1 John 5:4, preached in the small Dutch town of Kampen on Sunday, June 30, 1901. Viewed from theology-in-history, this sermon takes place at a fascinating moment in the Netherlands and in Bavinck's life. First, by 1901, Bavinck was an established public intellectual serving as a professor at the Theological University in Kampen, and he had recently completed the final volume of the first edition of his major theological work *The Reformed Dogmatics*. Moreover, he had been involved in a church unification process between two groups that had left the Dutch National Church. While not free from sorrow or struggle, there was much for Bavinck to celebrate by 1901. Furthermore, two weeks prior to this sermon the general election for the House of Representatives had taken place in the Netherlands, resulting in the anti-Revolutionary party founded on neo-Calvinist principles led by Abraham Kuyper who was asked to form a coalition government. Kuyper would become Prime Minister of the Netherlands in August 1901. Added to this, in the congregation that morning was the President of the South African Republic (Transvaal), Paul Krueger—who was a leader in the Second Boer War in South Africa, which was still ongoing when Bavinck delivered his sermon.

From the standpoint of theology-in-history, if any of Bavinck's sermons on 1 John 5:4 could take a triumphalist tone, it would be this one. However,

---

7. See Kuyper, *Problem of Poverty*.

8. For an excellent introduction to the contours of neo-Calvinist theology see Brock and Sutanto, *Neo-Calvinism*.

it is the context and Bavinck's response that makes this sermon appealing, fascinating, and illuminating. While Bavinck's sermon does have a political tone, underneath the surface of the political elements, the sermon presents a profound theological vision of God's restorative grace in Christ by the Spirit coming to renew the ruined creation as far as the curse is found (in all pervasive and polluting effects) and what it looks like to live and die in the comfort of belonging to Christ.[9] As such, the sermon itself not only serves as a great summary of Bavinck's entire theological vision, but it also serves as a kind of historical artifact, illuminating Bavinck's vision at work.

Bavinck begins his sermon with a direct appeal to the tumultuous nature of the previous century and the potential promise held out by current events:

> The nineteenth century, which lies only a few months behind us, has rightly been named by many as the century of unbelief and revolution. But although we have barely entered the twentieth century, we feel the question rise up within us involuntarily: might this new century allow us to see a return to the Christian faith and application of the principles of the Reformation to every area of life?[10]

Why might there be hope for the twentieth century? Bavinck goes on to identify three reasons: First, the revolutions of the eighteenth century and the reign of reason failed to deliver on their promises of a better world. Rather, their promises came back empty and void, leaving people tired and empty. According to Bavinck, this dissatisfaction opened a path for faith to speak to weary souls once again. Second, Bavinck notes the sacrifice for the sake of justice he sees displayed in the Boers against the English in South Africa.[11] Finally, he notes the recent victory of the Anti-Revolutionary Party.

Opening with an optimistic tone, Bavinck wonders with the congregation whether the neo-Calvinist vision for the Netherlands will come to fruition in the twentieth century. However, while Bavinck does mention the Boers twice again in the sermon, he never again specifically mentions the political victory gained at the polls, even if his congregation might have heard echoes of it in his language. Moreover, his subsequent mentions of the Boer War demonstrate that this sermon is no mere rallying cry for those who sought political, economic, or social "victory." Rather, Bavinck's true aim is to point his listeners to Christ as the one who has overcome a world of darkness and evil,

---

9. Language borrowed from Question 1 of the Heidelberg Catechism.

10. Bavinck, "World-Conquering Power," 67.

11. Bavinck's historical reference here concerning the recent events in South Africa is questionable. Furthermore, although Bavinck's praise of the Boers should be addressed, Bavinck was a child of his time, and he could not have foreseen the injustices that would unfold in South Africa in the latter half of the twentieth century.

"destruction and death," by his work on the cross, who is currently reigning over all things, and whose return will make all things new.[12] In other words, Bavinck seeks to invite his congregation to understand the current events within the context of broader theological affirmations.

To do this, Bavinck draws on the militaristic language and metaphors of Scripture in order to weave a picture of how faith is a gift by which believers "rest on [Christ's] victory" and "enter into [Christ's] work."[13] As he does, he roots himself deeply within the tradition of the Reformers, who sought to call believers to look to Christ, but he does so with a particularly neo-Calvinist accent.

For Bavinck, 1 John 5:4 encapsulates the scope of God's love and the universality of Christ's work. The "world" that John describes in this text, according to Bavinck, is not creation in all its beauty, richness, harmony, and goodness, but that which "stands against God" and "lies in evil . . . lives in a state of injustice . . . forms a kingdom of sin and unrighteousness . . . and . . . seeks to triumph over God by violence and trickery."[14] The "world," for Bavinck, is the misery and pollution that has invaded "every square inch" of God's good creation. While at war with God and standing in opposition to him, this is the very world God loves. Here the stark militaristic language Bavinck employs serves to highlight the beauty and scope of God's love: it is the love of an enemy to the utmost. Because God loves his world, even as it lives in opposition to him, in Christ, he overcomes the powers of sin, death, and destruction "as far as the curse is found" in order to restore and renew it. Only faith, then, can overcome the world because its content and object is Christ. Faith implants a new principle of life that renews from the inside out.

Victory, then, for Bavinck, does not look like a triumphant culture warrior—to use contemporary language—but rather it is the gift of new life, restoration, and wholeness. Furthermore, the new life that comes from the gift of faith, as Bavinck proclaims at the beginning and end of his sermon, is multiform. Toward the beginning of his sermon, Bavinck identifies three realities about faith: first and foremost, faith "implants a new principle of living in the person," moving someone from darkness to light.[15] As such, it transforms believers from the inside out, bringing with it "a mighty power toward love and obedience to God's commands."[16] Finally, faith, for Bavinck,

---

12. Bavinck, "World-Conquering Power," 75.
13. Bavinck, "World-Conquering Power," 83.
14. Bavinck, "World-Conquering Power," 73.
15. Bavinck, "World-Conquering Power," 70.
16. Bavinck, "World-Conquering Power," 70.

is not restricted to the interior life, but it is for all of life; Christ's redemption is cosmic in scope.

Returning to these concepts at the end of his sermon, Bavinck marks out the contours of faith's victory even more clearly. Faith's victory graciously brings believers into fellowship with God and gives peace and comfort to world-weary souls. However, it is not a faith that "withdraw[s] into the stillness of isolation, but rather it is living and power and breaks into the world.... It does not only enjoy; it works; it says something, and it does something."[17] What does it do? It witnesses, works, and acts. To explain this, Bavinck takes up a theme that can be seen throughout his writings in which he articulates the benefits of Christ's redemption through using the *munus triplex*, Christ's threefold office. This concept states that as sin is guilt, misery, and pollution, so Christ restores believers' relationship with God as prophet, renews the image in believers as priest, and preserves believers' heavenly inheritance as king. Moreover, in redemption, believers are anointed into these offices:

- As prophets, believers bear witness to the past work of Christ,
- As priests, believers look upward to see Christ seated at the right hand of God interceding for us.
- As kings, believers look forward to Christ's coming again when he will "put all his enemies under his feet and deliver the kingdom to God the Father."[18]

So too, in this sermon, Bavinck draws on the prophetic, priestly, and kingly roles given through Christ. Starting with the prophetic role, Bavinck notes that believers "bear witness that Jesus is the Christ."[19] Strikingly, here in the middle of a sermon which could sound optimistic and militaristic, Bavinck identifies martyrdom as that which bears the strongest witness to the reality that Christ alone is the Savior of the world. Moving onto the priestly and kingly roles, Bavinck identifies a few things that are worth noting. First, the fruit of faith is loving action. Faith "works through love" in the world.[20] Faith does not stop at bearing witness but is expressed in outward acts of self-giving love, fighting against the death, destruction, and dehumanizing consequences of sin. Faith does not act from itself but from "Christ alone."[21] As such, it "points to him . . .

---

17. Bavinck, "World-Conquering Power," 79.
18. Bavinck, *Reformed Dogmatics*, 3:594–95.
19. Bavinck, "World-Conquering Power," 81.
20. Bavinck, "World-Conquering Power," 81.
21. Bavinck, "World-Conquering Power," 81.

and depends on him."²² Even as faith manifests itself, working through love, it remains tethered to Christ. Implicit within Bavinck's language is a reminder that human action does not instantiate the kingdom of God, nor does it bring it to fulfillment. Believers await the final day when Christ will bring the kingdom in all its fullness as a part of their kingly office on earth. This call to live in anticipation and hope is strikingly present in Bavinck's sermon, which ends with the following words: "Come, then, Lord Jesus, yes, come quickly! Amen."²³

The bookends of Bavinck's sermon reveal a crucial aspect of Bavinck's theological vision. Starting with optimism derived from current events, Bavinck ends with hope derived from Christ's coming again, thereby transforming the way the congregation perceives current events. They are, at best, provisional signs of the kingdom, whose fullness is yet to come.

Bavinck's Theological Vision: Backward and Forward

As Bavinck's sermon on June 30, 1901, on 1 John 5:4 expressed his theological vision during a time when the neo-Calvinistic perspective seemed to be coming into full view, he also employed this vision in the midst of other, less optimistic times.

The Catholicity of Christianity

On December 30, 1888, Bavinck delivered an address at the Theological School in Kampen titled "The Catholicity of Christianity and the Church." Of particular note is that Bavinck gives this address in the midst of trying to secure a union between his church, which had seceded from the Dutch National Church in 1834, and the churches that had left the Dutch National Church in 1886 under the leadership of Kuyper. In this address, Bavinck argues that the catholicity of the church is threefold. First, the church is catholic because it is one unified whole in Christ. Individual churches are catholic insofar as they are united to the one universal church. Second, the church is catholic because it is "inclusive of believers from every nation, in all times and places."²⁴ And third, it is catholic because it "embraces the whole of human experience."²⁵ Interestingly, as he unpacks the third sense in which the faith is

---

22. Bavinck, "World-Conquering Power," 81.
23. Bavinck, "World-Conquering Power," 83.
24. Bavinck, "Catholicity," 221.
25. Bavinck, "Catholicity," 221.

catholic, Bavinck appeals to 1 John 5:4. Arguing against the isolationism and pietism he perceived within his own denomination but also painting a positive picture, Bavinck develops an account of the triune God's redemption that is cosmic in scope:

> Christianity knows no boundaries beyond those which God himself has in his good pleasure established; no boundaries of race or age, class, or status, nationality, or language. Sin has corrupted much; in fact, everything. The guilt of human sin is immeasurable; the pollution that always accompanies it penetrates every structure of humanity and the world. Nonetheless sin does not dominate and corrupt without God's abundant grace in Christ triumphing even more (Rom 5:15–20). The blood of Christ cleanses us from all sin; it is able to restore everything. We need not, indeed we must not, despair of anyone or anything. The Gospel is a joyful tiding, not only for the individual person but also for humanity, for the family, for society, for the state, for art and science, for the entire cosmos, for the whole groaning creation.[26]

It is a beautiful statement of the scope of God's redemptive love. Furthermore, the universality of Christianity extends through time. For Bavinck, "faith . . . can enter into all situations, connect with all forms of natural life, is suitable to every time, and beneficial for all things, and is relevant in all circumstances."[27] Why? Because according to Bavinck, "no matter how complicated the relationships may be within which we as Christ-confessors find ourselves in our age . . . faith has the promise of overcoming the world."[28] For Bavinck, Christ's redemption extends to the ends of creation and through history, manifesting itself in particular times and places. Thus, the Christian faith has something to say to every age—not just generally, but specifically. Each generation, then, is called to discern how the gospel both subverts and fulfills cultural presuppositions and longings.

Looking to this sermon, it is possible to see how he puts this theological affirmation into practice. Bavinck reads the landscape of his world in light of the world-conquering power of faith, which manifests itself in outward works of love, and waits in hope for the final day. The result? Optimism is transformed into hope and current events are placed within a broader gospel narrative.

---

26. Bavinck, "Catholicity," 224.
27. Bavinck, "Catholicity," 249.
28. Bavinck, "Catholicity," 249.

"Christianity"

Twenty-five years after "The Catholicity of Christianity" and eleven years after his sermon in 1901, Bavinck's context had significantly changed. Now living in Amsterdam, he described his current context as having moved from the "Age of Renan" (reason) to the "Age of Nietzsche." The hope of the neo-Calvinist future has fizzled, and Dutch society had become increasingly pluralistic and not necessarily troubled by the multiplicity of various, often incommensurate, world- and life-views. In this context, in 1912, Bavinck wrote "Christianity" as a part of a series introducing the various religions to the Dutch public.

Perhaps the most striking element of this work, in relation to the path traced thus far, is that it maintains the sense of Bavinck's earlier affirmations of faith's victory over the world, but now primarily through the language of rest. Particularly, in the last chapter of "Christianity," Bavinck focuses on the respite of Christianity, even as he acknowledges criticisms that Christianity and the church have done more harm than good. In a deeply Augustinian appeal through neo-Calvinist eyes, Bavinck writes:

> Humanity may progress along its course, but man always remains the same, his nature appears to be the same everywhere, and his heart can only be satisfied by God. . . . If there is to be any talk of comfort and peace for mankind, then this just and holy God must also be a merciful and gracious father who reconciles and forgives out of grace . . . who . . . in the course of regeneration and sanctification, transforms the world and mankind into a kingdom of God.[29]

The major theme is not changed here, but it is transposed into a different key. Now Bavinck emphasizes the rest that can only come from Christ because only he can satisfy the needs of the human heart. For all the critiques of Christianity, Bavinck still holds that faith is the victory that overcomes the world. Why? Because faith is what tethers believers to Christ.

Separated by over twenty-five years and in three distinct contexts, Bavinck's theological vision was formed by his deep theological and biblical articulation of the work of Christ, the inherent goodness of creation, the pervasiveness of sin, the triune God's work of recreation, and the firm belief that the good news of the gospel has something to say to every era. The values of this vision animated his response to his shifting context. Notwithstanding the reality that Bavinck's thought is not static, he draws on his theology to constructively respond to particular realities. To use contemporary language, Bavinck's theological commitments animated his theological imagination to

---

29. Bavinck, *What Is Christianity*, 60.

respond in rooted, constructive, and creative ways to the shifts of the latter half of the nineteenth and early twentieth centuries.

Seeing Through Bavinckian Eyes

While Bavinck belongs to a different era, he can help as a guide within our contemporary landscape by informing our theological imaginations as we wander in lands that used to seem familiar. Before proceeding, however, it is important to note that Bavinck is helpful not because he provides easy or specific answers to the challenges of twenty-first-century ecclesial life. Rather, Bavinck invites us into a theological framework that can form our intuitions and theological imaginations to respond today. Our theological imaginations contain intuitions rooted in theological commitments that direct the way we will respond to the myriad of challenges in our current landscape, our current liminal space. For example, an imagination that is formed by a conflation of Scripture and cultural conceptions of masculinity is less likely to be open to entering into conversations with women who have been deeply hurt by this conflation or even be less likely to hear Scripture's conceptualization of the church as the bride of Christ. A theological imagination formed by a bifurcation between evangelism and justice is less likely to see conversations pertaining to unjust structures and efforts to bring justice as crucial to the work of the church (locally and nationally). Contemporary evangelical theological imaginations are often marked by dichotomies such as evangelism vs. social action or justice, personal vs. systemic or systematic evil and sin, individual vs. communal, piety vs. activism, etc. As a theologian from a different era, Bavinck often holds together what has been torn asunder in today's ecclesial contexts, thereby inviting us to bind together what contemporary dichotomies have rent apart.

Furthermore, as a voice from the past, Bavinck helps restore a historical consciousness to the evangelical theological imagination. This is not the first time, nor will it be the last, the church has faced significant challenges and a shifting context. Bavinck reminds contemporary readers that the church prevails through the ages, not because of her ingenuity but because she is a body founded and kept safe by Christ.

Bavinck also invites contemporary believers to ground their theological imaginations in the firm conviction that the good news of the gospel is cosmic in scope and aimed at the full restoration and redemption of this world. For Bavinck, the triune God undoes the havoc that sin has wrought personally and communally in all its dehumanizing and polluting ways. It is this gospel, according to Bavinck, that speaks to the ills and challenges of every age. It brings real hope and life, not just to individuals but to communities, as faith works through love, refusing to forsake action in this world, even as it stands in hopeful expectation of the world to come. For in beholding Christ, the author and perfector of our faith, we behold the one who has, in Bavinck's words, "overcome the world."

But how does this really help? How does this help in the midst of real ecclesial challenges? Is this not just an overly simplistic appeal to look to Christ? However, it is here that Bavinck's approach can be deeply comforting. Even in the midst of "success," he implores believers to look to Christ and remember that all efforts, even those that bring needed justice and healing, are provisional signs that bear witness to the coming kingdom. In liminal spaces, we need guides, but we also need a tether, and Bavinck tethers us, not to a particular event or program, but to Christ and the hope of his coming kingdom.

It is in tethering us to Christ that Bavinck can inject hope into evangelical theological imaginations. Hope gives believers and leaders assurance from which to respond without anxiety. There is a growing body of helpful and insightful literature on how self-differentiation is an essential component of nonanxious leadership within liminal spaces. Bavinck adds to this discussion with a specifically theological contribution. His contribution is less about learning to be a self-differentiated leader and more about being a leader who knows that the gospel is good news "no matter how serious and difficult, perhaps even insoluble, the problems may seem in the areas of society, politics, and above all [in scholarship]."[30] From this firm knowledge of the good news of God in Christ, Bavinck forms believers to find rest and hope for our souls. Even if our actions now in "reconstructing" end in what feels like defeat, the promise of Christ's coming reign still holds. As Bavinck notes in his sermon on 1 John 5:4, we cannot mechanize our way to "success"; sometimes Christian witness to the gospel ends in giving up everything. Nevertheless, the hope of the Christian life is not in finding the right ingredients to assure the ascendancy of one's church, political party, or social cause to temporal triumph. Rather, the hope of the church is found in Christ and following him, and the calling of the pastor theologian is to steward/guide the congregation to this end. To do so in a culture where we may expect to win or in which we believe we have to win at all costs calls for not merely stating this reality but finding the way to unearth this reality in the lives of our congregants in liturgy, story, song, etc.

In tethering believers to Christ and injecting hope through faith, Bavinck is helpful again because, in his work, nonanxious never means nonactive. In Bavinck, the faith which births hope is not something that withdraws from engagement in the world. Rather, it acts in love. Also,to act in love is to love as Jesus did, welcoming the sinners, engaging them where they are, seeking to

---

30. Bavinck, "Catholicity," 249.

understand their life, heart, pain, etc. Jesus's love for the sinner (vs. his calling out the religious leaders) needs to shape and mold us.

Applied to our own context, then, a theological imagination formed in part by Bavinck's theological vision is one that enters into the messy world within our churches to seek justice and love mercy, sits with the victims and listens to their stories, and seeks to respond in ways that do not sweep things under the rug because of fear that it will ruin someone's or the institution's reputation. Rather, tethered to Christ, leaders can steward their congregations through these challenging realities, knowing that faith works to overcome real darkness in the world by naming sin and working in love to make it right while hoping for the final day.

Finally, as a guide alongside other theologians, philosophers, psychologists, and people from other fields, Bavinck can aid those who lead in the complex and marred context of American ecclesial life. Bavinck aids us by helping our evangelical imaginations to move in a particular direction even though he may not give specific answers. For Bavinck, the gospel is good news in this life and the next. It alone provides rest for weary souls, not just for those within the church who are burning out and filled with sorrow but also for those who are seeking rest elsewhere, whether it be in the next political election, a particular social cause, their vocation, experiences, or something else. For Bavinck, because Christ alone gives rest to restless souls, we can look out at the world and, though frustrated, annoyed, and exhausted, learn to see beneath the surface to wounded and weary souls who are scared and searching for that which will fulfill them.

Bibliography

Bavinck, Herman. "The Catholicity of Christianity and the Church." Translated by John Bolt. *CTJ* 27.2 (1992) 220–51.

———. *Herman Bavinck on Preaching and Preachers*. Translated and edited by James Eglinton. Peabody, MA: Hendrickson, 2021.

———. *Reformed Dogmatics*. 4 vols. Edited by John Bolt. Translated by John Vriend. Grand Rapids: Baker, 2003–8.

———. *What Is Christianity?* Translated and edited by Gregory Parker Jr. Peabody, MA: Hendrickson Academic, 2022.

———. "World-Conquering Power of Faith." In *Herman Bavinck on Preaching and Preachers*, translated and edited by James P. Eglinton, 67–84. Peabody, MA: Hendrickson, 2017.

Beaumont, Susan. *How to Lead When You Don't Know Where You're Going: Leading in a Liminal Season*. London: Rowman and Littlefield, 2019.

Brock, Cory C., and N. Gray Sutanto. *Neo-Calvinism: A Theological Introduction*. Bellingham, WA: Lexham Academic, 2023.

Friedman, Edwin H. *A Failure of Nerve*. New York: Seabury, 2007.
Kuyper, Abraham. *The Problem of Poverty*. Translated by James W. Silken. Sioux Center, IA: Dordt College Press, 2011.
Molendijk, Arie L. *Protestant Theology and Modernity in the Nineteenth-Century Netherlands*. Oxford: Oxford University Press, 2022.
Sayers, Mark. *A Non-Anxious Presence: How a Changing and Complex World Will Create a Remnant of Renewed Christian Leaders*. Chicago: Moody, 2022.
Taylor, Charles. *A Secular Age*. Cambridge, MA: Belknap, 2007.

8

Mission After Evangelicalism

MICHAEL NIEBAUER

Introduction

MISSION IN CONTEMPORARY AMERICAN Evangelicalism is hindered by its fixation on growth and influence. Its mission practitioners are indebted to a model of mission that posits numerical growth as its ultimate goal. However, since the fastest way to start and grow churches in America is through the recruitment of financially stable Christians, American Evangelicalism has developed a culture that disincentivizes church planters from focusing their efforts on the poor and lost. Furthermore, evangelical mission is hindered by public discourse meant to bolster the reputation of Christianity through rhetorical acts of dissociation, in which individuals constantly identify and separate themselves from those Christians whom they disagree with. However, such rhetorical acts are largely ineffective and obscure the need to proclaim the gospel among those in the perceived out group.

A recovery and renewal of evangelical mission should come instead by conceiving of mission as a virtuous craft whose telos is not numerical growth but the glory of God. Such a conception of mission backgrounds public reputational discourse and foregrounds private persuasive communication.

In what follows I will offer a critique of mission in contemporary American Evangelicalism, beginning with an assessment of the problems associated with Evangelicalism's fixation on growth and influence. Following these critiques, I posit a constructive path forward in mission, taking as a starting point my positive construal of mission as virtuous practice developed in my book *Virtuous Persuasion*.

Mission as Growth

The first major issue within American Evangelicalism is its fixation on mission as church growth. The principal means by which American Evangelicalism conceives of mission is through the successful planting of new congregations and the numerical increase in weekly attendance of existing congregations. This model of mission has its roots in Donald McGavran's Church Growth movement of the 1960s and 1970s, which was then domesticated and transformed into the church planting movements of the 1990s up until today. In *Virtuous Persuasion* I detail several key aspects of this model.[1] First: growth is the goal of mission. This is considered intuitive by many contemporary Evangelicals: if I am responsible for mission, I am more successful when I plant more churches and have more people attending my churches and less successful when my attendance figures drop. The second aspect is that such growth is predictable: there are specific methods of evangelism and church planting that lead to growth, and such methods can be discovered, studied, and replicated. The burgeoning industry of church growth and church planting books is in part predicated upon this assumption: the successful church planter documents their story of growth and the methods they deployed that helped bring about this growth, with the hope that others might read, replicate, and experience a similar amount of growth.

A key to understanding the issues involved in this conception of mission is to examine the persons targeted by the church growth movement. For heuristic purposes, we can identify three major groups of people in America. First, there are practicing Christians who, for a multitude of reasons, are looking for a local church community. As a highly mobile society, mission in the United States has included some form of outreach to, or gathering of, these persons. Provided individuals have appropriate reasons for looking for a church, a missionary who attempts to gather such persons is providing a necessary good.

Second, there are the so-called "nominal Christians," those with some Christian background but who do not attend church or religious events frequently. While many Evangelicals would state that such persons need to be converted, it is better to describe such persons as those in need of revival.

---

1. Niebauer, *Virtuous Persuasion*, 41–50.

Though the language of evangelism and conversion are used often, mission throughout the history of American Protestantism has principally been concerned with this group of people. Since the majority of Americans have had at least some Christian background, and self-identify as Christian, the job of the revivalist has been to activate, to revive, and to awaken in such persons the true content of their nominal faith. In this way, the work of American Evangelicalism has more in common with medieval mendicant preaching than it does with foreign missions in pagan territories.

The third group are those who are explicitly not Christian, whether adherents of a different religion, or atheist or agnostic. Although this has been a very small group throughout American history, it has been steadily rising over the past decades. Outreach to those who are explicitly non-Christian has historically been called missionary work, but has been the focus of relatively few Evangelicals throughout American history.

We can now see how the mission-as-growth model intersects with these different groups of persons. As it emerged in American Evangelicalism in the seventies, eighties, and nineties, the mission-as-growth model fit reasonably well with revivalism. Most Americans had some basic understanding of the Christian faith and a familiarity with Christian concepts and biblical characters. This general understanding of Christianity made possible large and effective acts of public persuasion aimed at reviving and accelerating this base knowledge. It allowed enthymematic persuasion—one could use words like grace, faith, and salvation without having to render such words intelligible to a broad audience.

Because of this general understanding of Christianity and the large number of persons who attended church at least sporadically in their lifetime, church growth experts could utilize broad and highly strategic methods in order to attract people to a new or existing church. The structure and style of a church service could then be tailored to meet the expectations of these persons. The rise of Willow Creek Church is the most prominent example of large-scale appeals to those in need of revival. Bill Hybels developed door-to-door surveys which asked individuals if they currently attend church, and, if the answer was no, asked for reasons why. The church services and marketing campaigns at Willow Creek were then tailored to the results of this survey.[2] Such surveys are predicated on a revivalist mentality. They assume a general background understanding of the Christian faith and assume that churchgoing is an activity that most Americans have engaged in at some point in their life.

However, changes in the religious composition of the United States over the past twenty years has made the success of the mission-as-growth model

---

2. Pritchard, *Willow Creek Seeker Services*, 75.

suspect. There has been a rise in the number of people who are not Christian and a decline in the number of persons with some form of Christian background. There are fewer people in need of revival and more people in need of full-scale conversion. This poses a problem when growth is the goal of mission, since those with no Christian background are typically unresponsive to large-scale outreach. Advertisements with words such as "abundant grace" and "new life" have become largely unintelligible to a large swath of Americans. Such persons cannot be reached with direct marketing. Instead, the missionary is required to spend large amounts of time and effort to reach such people: they must develop individual relationships, engage in multiple spiritual conversations, none of which guarantees that an individual will ever darken the door of the church.

With fewer nominal Christians in need of revival, the church planter increasingly has only one group of individuals who will be responsive to their broad-based strategies of growth: those who are already active Christians. This is the last remaining group of individuals who are shopping for new churches, who are perusing church websites, and who are open to the persuasion of mass-market advertisements. And so the church planting enterprise becomes one of gathering Christians disaffected with their current church and those who are residentially mobile. It is primarily about gathering, rather than reviving or converting. This helps to explain the success of the church growth model in new suburbs in the 1980s and 1990s and in large urban centers in the first decades of the twenty-first century: these are the areas with the greatest influx of upwardly mobile Christians, and hence the easiest places to start and grow new churches.

So the church planter must choose between achieving rapid growth by reaching existing Christians or slow or nonexistent growth through reaching non-Christians. But the commitment to numerical growth as the telos of mission means that one must choose the former even if, ironically, it means committing to a kind of Evangelicalism that involves no actual evangelism. Those who attempt to deviate from this norm—to start new churches and ministries that engage those who are explicitly not Christian—will find a number of obstacles due to the incentive structures built into an evangelical culture steeped in the language of church growth. First, there are financial incentives to engaging in church planting that is centered upon the gathering of wealthy Christians. Since, in most evangelical contexts, church finances are tethered to congregational giving, the church planter will find that the quickest way to financial security will come by growing a church as quickly as possible, and by attracting Christians who are wealthy. This goes hand in hand with a focus on the upwardly mobile—Christians who are moving to a new town typically have the education and means to move to new towns and are thus prime targets for the upstart church planter.

In addition to financial incentives, there are also professional incentives to grow a church as fast as possible, and hence to focus one's efforts on attracting Christians as opposed to non-Christians. The successful missionary is the builder of the large church full of young successful difference-makers and culture-shapers. They are rewarded for their success with greater prestige in their denominations and book contracts from Christian publishers.

The incentive structure of American Evangelicalism thus rewards those who pursue the gathering of wealthy, upwardly mobile Christians into churches and disincentivizes the slower missionary work of reaching non-Christians, and the less lucrative missionary work of reaching the poor and outcast. If one starts a church of 300 college graduates in the Lincoln Park neighborhood of Chicago, one will receive more wealth and prestige as opposed to starting a church of fifty persons in a nursing home in rural West Virginia.

I have elaborated further on incentive structures in order to demonstrate that the mission-as-growth model is still deeply ingrained in the culture of American Evangelicalism. While there have been more voices opposing this fixation on numbers in recent years, the incentive structures have not changed. The effects of this model are felt anytime a pastor's emotional well-being is tethered to the ups and downs of Sunday attendance. It is felt anytime a church planter raises money and is asked by donors for data on the size of their church. It is evident in a celebrity culture that rewards numerically successful church planters with book contracts and professional advancement while obscuring the skilled yet less fruitful evangelism done among the lost and obscure.

Mission and Reputation

The other major issue within American Evangelicalism concerns its fixation on reputation and influence. The evangelical movement has historically sought not only the conversion of souls but the increased influence of Evangelicalism on the broader American culture. Part of the rationale for the attainment of this influence was missional: the more American culture reflected Christian values and the better the reputation of Evangelicals, the easier it would be to share the gospel.

Recently, this fixation on reputation has been made manifest through the engagement of large numbers of evangelical pastors, theologians, and laypersons in acts of public dissociation in the service of Christian mission. Dissociation is a rhetorical term used to describe the ways that individuals, through the use of speech, attempt to create separation between thought and person, and individual from group. It is the process by which one attempts to define an in-group as opposed to an out-group. One of the purposes of such acts is to better define one's particular group for the sake of group cohesion. Groups must decide what they stand for and expel those who do not uphold specific group values. This type of work is done, often in private, within evangelical churches and universities: one must define and interpret statements of faith and discern who is in and who is out.

But one of the other purposes, specifically of *public* dissociative speech, is to bolster the prestige of the rhetor's particular group. One wants both a well-defined group and a group that has a favorable opinion within the broader society. Such prestige can "promote the spread of its ideas, habits, and customs and of its products and methods; everyone knows that hostility felt toward a group can become a serious handicap to the spread of these things."[3] The more prestige and less hostility that a specific group has in the eyes of the larger community, the greater its ability to promote its ideas and values.

Such acts of dissociation meant to bolster prestige are now a common feature of evangelical public discourse. There is currently an ongoing public battle taking place online and in the pulpits over a number of terms and definitions, with numerous pastors, theologians, and lay Christians attempting to separate Christian nationalism from Evangelicalism, or Evangelicalism from Christianity, or woke evangelical from evangelical. In each of these acts, the speaker defines the in-group as representing what we can call "true Christianity" and the out-group as representing those ideas that are a part of "false Christianity."

The purpose of this dissociative public discourse is in part to bolster the reputation of the in-group on behalf of the broader public, either for the purpose of acquiring more influence within the broader culture or for making Christianity more amenable to those outside of the faith. No one wishes to begin an evangelistic encounter by digging oneself out of a reputational ditch, and the greater respectability of Christianity, the greater the opportunity to effectively share the gospel.

Such acts of dissociation are not new within the evangelical movement, though through much of the twentieth century the arguments were conducted mostly among evangelical elites concerned about distinctions between fundamentalism and modernism, or ideas such as biblical inerrancy. However, the twenty-first century has seen a large expansion in the number of people compelled to engage in dissociative public discourse, as well as the number of events that compel those speakers to engage.

3. Perelman and Olbrechts-Tyteca, *New Rhetoric*, 322.

PART TWO: OPPORTUNITIES

Bradford Vivian chronicles the expansion of the range and scope of events that now elicit broad public response. A century ago, this compulsion to publicly respond to events was limited to direct participants in traumatic experiences—we can think here of the need for holocaust survivors to publicize their stories. Now, however, one is compelled to respond to *all* public events, no matter how trivial, and no matter whether one is a direct participant in those events.[4] And this is precisely what is occurring whenever a pastor or theologian consumes a piece of news concerning Evangelicalism. A feeling of obligation, of the need to speak out, overcomes the reader, and in response a statement is composed, a tweet is sent, or a sermon is written. Each person takes upon themselves the burden of entering into public discourse in order to dissociate specific persons or ideas from true Christianity in order to save the reputation of the church.

As stated above, such acts of dissociation are not necessarily wrong—every group must define what they believe and which persons adhere to their beliefs. What is new, however, is the *intensity* and *ubiquity* of these acts of dissociation: all are now compelled to engage in public discourse for the sake of Christianity's reputation. Reputation guarding becomes a kind of missional imperative for evangelical Christians. One perceives Christian nationalism or woke Evangelicalism as a constant threat to the health and vitality of American Christianity, a threat that must be constantly and publicly condemned lest the gospel message be compromised.

While frequently deployed to bolster the reputation of Christianity for the sake of its mission, such dissociative acts can tend to have a detrimental effect on the individuals who deploy such speech. Acts of speech impact both the speaker and their audience. In our attempts to influence the world around us through the use of speech, we are inevitably changed. Speech transforms both speaker and audience, and my contention is that these acts of dissociation can malform the speaker, training them to view those in the supposed out group as simplistic and coherent wholes, which "unself-consciously distorts the realities of lived practice."[5] Here I am adopting a critique of modern anthropology articulated by Kathryn Tanner. According to Tanner, the modern anthropologist, in the interest of discovering consistent and reliable data, looks to discover a deep unity within specific cultures based upon observable beliefs and practices. Such classifications, however, paper over the exceptions to these unified cultures, and fail to grapple with the lived experiences of individual recipients of the anthropologist's cultural monikers.

---

4. Vivian, *Commonplace Witnessing*, 10.
5. Tanner, *Theories of Culture*, 42.

I believe something akin to this happens when Evangelicals engage in public acts of dissociation. Such acts train the participants to think of "Christian nationalists" or "woke Evangelicals" as discreet wholes, as well as ascribing a meaning to the actions of these persons that neglects the lived experiences of the individual. So, for instance, one attempts to dissociate themselves from "white Evangelicals" for their support of Donald Trump, based upon polling that shows that 80 percent of self-described white Evangelicals voted for Donald Trump in the 2020 election. However, such distancing oversimplifies and overinterprets the lived experiences of individual voters. First, it papers over the 20 percent who did not vote for Trump. But more importantly, it refuses to tend to the multitude of reasonings behind each individual act of voting. Some may have voted for Trump enthusiastically, others reluctantly. Some may have done so with little deliberation and moved on with their lives.

In addition, the labeling of white Evangelicals itself distorts the lived reality of those who self-describe in such a way. One of the most striking points of recent data involves the decline in frequency of church attendance of self-described Evangelicals, and the rise in the number of self-described Evangelicals who seldom if ever attend church.[6] The semantic range of the term "evangelical" seems to be evolving—rising in its application to a kind of cultural heritage and declining as a term that denotes religious fervor. Thus, to speak of a discreet whole of "white Evangelicals" obscures the speaker to the reality that many white Evangelicals are actually persons in need of revival, in need of the gospel, and in need of being born again. A person who once was considered to be nominal in their faith and in need of the gospel witness is now labeled a religious heretic, worthy of judgment and excommunication.

Those whose mission is to save the reputation of Christianity through public acts of dissociation are in danger of developing hardened hearts to those perceived as the out-group, whichever label such a group dons. Every day one consumes a range of information about the beliefs and actions of various Evangelicals. One is then compelled to publicly react to this information, positioning oneself as those for the in-group of true Christians and against the out-group of false Christians. They are then compelled to react even when the information they ingest has little bearing on their individual lives. Such disembodied reactions sediment beliefs about groups of people that do not reflect the lived experiences of individuals within these groups. Those within these groups that are in need of the gospel are written off. If mission is the movement of God toward the lost, and human participation in mission is the movement of Christians toward the lost, then the result of such endeavors is

---

6. Smith, "About Three-in-Ten U.S. Adults."

a kind of anti-mission. One sees the symbols and flags of the out-group, and immediately moves to public judgment and distance.

The question that one must ask themselves when they partake in these acts of dissociation is this: are such acts fostering in me a greater love of neighbor? Are my denouncements of Christian nationalists instilling in me a more loving heart for the nominal Christians living in Clearfield County, Pennsylvania? Are my denouncements of "woke" Christians instilling in me a greater love of urbane Manhattanites? Is such discourse enflaming in me a passion to enter into the lives of such persons with the hope of proclaiming the good news of Jesus Christ? If instead such acts drive me further away from such persons, then I am doing the work of anti-mission, of fleeing from Nineveh for the safer ground of Tarshish.

Because of its fixation on growth and reputation, there is little left of American Evangelicalism that is truly evangelical. The professional class of missionaries—now referred to as church planters and church growth experts—are engaged in the honing of techniques rendered not in the service of evangelism or revival, but instead in service to socially mobile Christians. At its best, these efforts provide solid churches for those who are new to an area or who, for legitimate reasons, must leave their current church. At its worst, it promotes and encourages committed Christians to constantly search for greener ecclesial pastures.

While the professional missionary class of Evangelicals is engaged in an incessant rearranging of the pews, other Evangelicals are engaged in a neverending quest to redefine the boundaries of American Christianity for the sake of restoring its reputation for the broader culture. Such reputation building, done through public acts of rhetorical dissociation, do not bolster the prestige of Christianity, since they are mostly ignored by the broader public. At its worst, such actions blind their propagators to the potential gospel witness that is still needed within members of their perceived out-group.

Mission After Evangelicalism

The above sections outlined some of the current problems with the state of mission within American Evangelicalism. In what follows I posit a handful of suggestions for contemporary mission within North America that address these issues. These suggestions proceed from the top down, from the theoretical to the practical, moving roughly along the lines of my constructive proposal of mission as virtuous practice as outlined in *Virtuous Persuasion*. In that book, I posit: *Christian mission is best construed as specific activities (proclamation and gathering) that develop virtue in its practitioners, moving them toward their ultimate goal of partaking in the glory of God.*[7] In what follows, I invite Evangelicals to enter into mission along these lines, moving from growth to glory and from public to private witness.

First, there is a movement from growth to glory. The ultimate goal of mission is not the numerical increase of specific churches or ministries but rather the glory of God. While the missionary strives to persuasively proclaim the gospel and adroitly gather new believers into a worshiping community, these are penultimate goals, subordinate to the true telos of missional activity, which is the beatific vision. While the missionary strives for excellence in the practical performances of proclamation and gathering, their goal is to honor and delight in God in the acts of mission themselves, regardless of results. There is a deep joy in beautifully presenting the good news of Jesus Christ to the lost and downtrodden. There is a deep joy in seeing the first fruits of communion spring up in a newly established congregation. Such joys can be experienced whether their interlocutors reject the gospel and whether their newly established church is but two or three gathered together in the name of Christ.

Establishing the glory of God as the goal of mission does not detract from the necessity of performing mission well. Since one desires to honor God with their words, they should strive to proclaim the gospel to the best of their abilities. According to Aquinas, all deliberate activity, when done in accordance with our true ends, is a participation in the Divine Essence.[8] This sets a high bar for mission, as it requires that the missionary reorient every aspect of their vocation toward this end. Every moment in prayer for the lost, every Bible study formed, every moment spent in conversation with a non-Christian, is done under the divine gaze, and as such should be performed to the best of one's abilities.

However, all proximate ends of mission, whether they be the numerical increase of the church or the bolstered reputation of Christianity within the broader culture, must be sacrificed if they conflict with this ultimate goal of glorifying God. Acts of proclamation that distort the gospel message in order to win adherents are *always* wrong whether they lead to numerical success or not. Public acts of dissociation meant to bolster the reputation of Evangelicalism are *always* wrong if they erode in their promulgator the love of neighbor. Numbers, power, prestige, influence, and reputation must *always* yield to faith, hope, and love.

Stephen's speech in Acts 7 is a vivid example of the missional practice of proclamation done in accordance with the ultimate goal of the beatific vision.

---

7. Niebauer, *Virtuous Persuasion*, 109–10.
8. Aquinas, *Summa Theologiae*, 1, q. 1.

Stephen gives an extraordinarily articulate and highly persuasive speech exhorting the crowd to believe in Jesus Christ as Lord and God. It is a brilliant display of theological acumen and rhetorical eloquence leveraged toward the penultimate goal of converting the masses. And yet, Stephen's speech is unflinching in its judgments on the crowd despite the crowd's growing anger. The potential for a large increase in converts and the bolstering of the prestige of Christianity are sacrificed in order that Stephen might be faithful to the message he is called to share. For this sacrifice and brilliant display of fortitude, he is rewarded by the crowd with stones, but by God with a vision of Jesus standing at the right hand of the Father.

Stephen is anathema to contemporary American Evangelicalism. Unlike Peter's actions, which produced thousands of converts, Stephen's speech resulted in negative growth—there was one less Christian after his speech concluded. There would be no books published unearthing his missionary secrets, no books inviting the reader to replicate his methods with guaranteed results. Furthermore, Stephen's caustic speech alienated his onlookers and diminished the prestige of Christianity within the broader culture. He was not rewarded with public approval or a favorable interview in the *New York Times*. However, Scripture shows that Stephen received the highest reward of any missionary in the Book of Acts—the beatific vision of Jesus, the same vision that Christians will receive on Mount Zion in the eschaton. Each and every act of mission that is done in the footsteps of Stephen pushes the missionary one step closer to this end.

Second, there is a movement from public to private witness. Evangelical mission is fixated on large-scale public appeals at a time in which such appeals are ineffective and/or counterproductive. While public acts of dissociation may marginally affect the reputation of Christians for the better, they risk flattening distinctions among individuals and hardening hearts toward those who may identify as Evangelical but still need to accept the gospel.

As outlined in *Virtuous Persuasion*, my description of the virtuous practice of proclamation foregrounds an embodied encounter with specific individuals and the cultivation of virtue within these encounters. The proclamation of the gospel is first and foremost an embodied encounter between a Christian and one or many non-Christians, in which an invitation is offered to follow Jesus as Lord and God.

Such encounters begin in prayer. Here, the missionary offers up before God their interlocutors, asking for the cultivation of the love of neighbor and a desire to see them enter into a relationship with God the Father, Son, and Holy Spirit. It is in prayer that my neighbor becomes more than a number, more than an anonymous person who could bolster the size of my ministry. Public dissociation trains the heart to see one's neighbor as a political partisan, whose yard signs and flags determine their amenability to the gospel. However, it is in prayer that the Holy Spirit grants a heart of flesh capable of seeing through the political proclivities of one's neighbor. In prayer the Holy Spirit fosters a love of neighbor, and since love moves the lover toward its object of love, this love propels the Christian to enter into the life of their neighbor, desiring for them to repent and believe in Christ's death and resurrection.

Love prompts one to proclaim the gospel, and this comes in the form of a dialogical encounter. Here, one must develop some degree of practical skill, learning how to articulate the Christian faith and discovering those aspects of the faith that will be persuasive within this encounter. The process of *inventio*, of discovering the available means of persuasion, prompts the missionary to consider both the challenges and opportunities afforded them by the unique personal beliefs and histories of those they encounter. Rather than dismiss outright certain political and cultural beliefs as placing an individual beyond the pale, the missionary looks for seeds of the gospel wherever they can. The Christian nationalist who has embraced God and country has at least some conception of God, which is a starting point for a discussion about the incarnation. The progressive donning a secular creed yard sign has already developed a sense of justice, of a creation that yearns for its proper order. Such beliefs can be the starting point for an invitation to understand him in whom all things hold and have their being.

It is here that some of the more practical resources on apologetics and evangelism can be helpful. However, because each opportunity to proclaim the gospel involves a unique and nonrepeatable encounter with a person, none of these resources guarantee replicable success. For this reason, the missionary must also cultivate the virtues, which are "dispositions to make choices which will make you better able to make choices."[9]

An example or two will help illustrate this conception of mission and virtue. For instance, in most circumstances, those engaged in mission must first establish relationships with those outside of the church. While one could glean a few tips for meeting new people through mission handbooks—for instance, how to get more involved in community events, how to strike up conversations with strangers, etc.—ultimately one will need to cultivate the virtue of friendliness in order to establish the type of meaningful relationships that are the foundation for most proclamations of the gospel. Friendliness cannot be learned through the acquisition of abstract knowledge in a manual, but instead must be cultivated through experience. One has to learn friendliness through being a friend and observing others who are adept at making new

9. McCabe, *Good Life*, 29.

friends. In so doing, they learn to avoid querulousness and obsequiousness—how to be pleasant and agreeable without being a pushover, and how to stand firm in what one believes without being grouchy.

Above friendliness is the virtue of prudence. A challenge faced by all those engaged in mission is to be loving and gracious in one's presentation of the gospel while also being unyielding in their commitment to the truths of the gospel. One is called to be loving in conversation with one's neighbor and courageous in the face of hostility from one's neighbor. Friendliness and fortitude must intertwine in the proclamative encounter, and prudence is the virtue that enables the missionary to discern with alacrity the proper proportion of each.

There are times for winsomeness and times for judgment. Neglecting prudence will inevitability lead to frivolous attempts to determine *a priori* the appropriateness of one or the other. Since each proclamation of the gospel is a unique event, it requires the missionary to discern within a lived encounter when to praise, when to challenge, and when to condemn.

Conclusion: My Prayer

My prayer for American Evangelicalism is that it would shake loose its fixations with growth and reputation and truly embrace the call to mission which all churches are called to in a pluralistic society like America. My prayer is that it would judge its success in mission not by the number of warm bodies in the pews, nor in its reputation amongst the broader culture, but instead by the number of its adherents who faithfully and beautifully proclaim the life, death, and resurrection of Christ whatever the earthly rewards, knowing that their heavenly reward, the glory of God, is secure.

Bibliography

Aquinas, Thomas. *Summa Theologica*. Translated by Fathers of the English Dominican Province. Notre Dame, IN: Christian Classics, 1948.

McCabe, Herbert. *The Good Life: Ethics and the Pursuit of Happiness*. London: Bloomsbury, 2005.

Niebauer, Michael. *Virtuous Persuasion: A Theology of Christian Mission*. Bellingham, WA: Lexham Academic, 2022.

Perelman, Chaïm, and Lucie Olbrechts-Tyteca. *The New Rhetoric: A Treatise on Argumentation*. Translated by John Wilkinson and Purcell Weaver. Notre Dame: University of Notre Dame Press, 1969.

Pritchard, G. A. *Willow Creek Seeker Services: Evaluating a New Way of Doing Church*. Grand Rapids, MI: Baker, 1996.

Tanner, Kathryn. *Theories of Culture: A New Agenda for Theology.* Minneapolis: Fortress, 1997.
Smith, Gregory A. "About Three-in-Ten U.S. Adults Are Now Religiously Unaffiliated." Pew Research Center, December 14, 2021. https://www.pewresearch.org/religion/2021/12/14/about-three-in-ten-u-s-adults-are-now-religiously-unaffiliated/.
Vivian, Bradford. *Commonplace Witnessing: Rhetorical Invention, Historical Remembrance, and Public Culture.* Oxford: Oxford University Press, 2017.

9

How Church History Can Help Us Reconstruct Evangelicalism

GAVIN ORTLUND

INTRODUCTION

HOW MIGHT CHURCH HISTORY help us reconstruct Evangelicalism? My argument here is that church history will encourage us toward even-handedness and sympathy in the process.

As a preacher, I am aware that it is always risky to reference any modern-day politician for any purpose whatsoever. Even if your point is not about politics, some people can get stuck there. So I beg you to consider the following illustration not as making a political point, but as making a more basic human and sociological point that will crack open this idea of *reconstruction*.

In March of 2008, during his presidential campaign, Barack Obama gave a speech entitled, "A More Perfect Union." The context was that Obama was responding to concerns about controversial remarks made by his pastor, Jeremiah Wright. In his presidential memoirs, Obama describes the intensity of the days leading up to that speech. At the time, it seemed like this episode might tank his whole campaign. He writes, "There are moments in politics, as in life . . . when the only option is to steel yourself and go for broke."[1] He

---

1. Obama, *Promised Land*, 141.

narrates staying up till 3 a.m. the night before, tweaking the speech. The mindset was, "We might lose the election for this, but at least I'll be saying what I believe."

In the speech, Obama condemned Rev. Wright's statements, but not his person. He emphasized the complexity of our racial heritage as a nation, and that we cannot simply dismiss the anger reflected in his remarks. Without condoning it, we need to *understand* it in order to make progress. And he said: "*These people are a part of me.* And they are part of America, *this* country that I love."[2]

One reason the speech was so effective is that Obama's critique of Wright was intermingled with a sense of *even-handedness and sympathy*. It was less like dropping a bomb, and more like a careful surgery.

My proposal is that in the project of reconstructing Evangelicalism, we need even-handedness and sympathy. Just as when you are counseling a friend who is struggling with addiction or depression, you are not well poised to help them unless you have some level of sympathy, so also we are not well poised to help a tradition (like Evangelicalism) if we have no sympathy for it. Sympathy does not mean condoning what is evil. It means understanding, carefulness, and love.

And without sympathy, we will often get stuck in deconstruction. Deconstruction is important, but it is not an end in itself. It serves the larger end of reconstruction. Only doing deconstruction without reconstruction is like if you bring your car to the mechanic, and he takes it apart, but does not put it back together. Then the car does not drive! Or it is like if you go to the doctor, and he gives a brilliant diagnosis, but does not give you any medicine. Then you do not get better! To work *through* deconstruction into *reconstructing* Evangelicalism, we need even-handedness and sympathy.

That is not easy. The pressures upon us in the current culture are away from even-handedness and sympathy and toward outrage and tribalism. So how do we do this?

One profoundly helpful tool is church history. Church history allows us to see contemporary Evangelicalism, with both its glories and warts, in a larger context. It reminds us that the task of reconstruction is an ancient and recurring one. So let us learn two lessons from church history: first, about the nature of reconstruction (i.e., *how* we reconstruct); second, about the goal of reconstruction (i.e., *what* we reconstruct).

---

2. Obama, "More Perfect Union," para. 24 (emphasis added).

PART TWO: OPPORTUNITIES

The Nature of Reconstruction

One of the most striking and sobering facts about church history is that there is always a poignant mixture of both good and bad, and thus, there will be a perennial temptation to focus on one to the neglect of the other. We can focus on the good to the neglect of the bad (leading to unhealthy idealism). Or we can focus on the bad to the neglect of the good (leading to an unhealthy cynicism). Reconstruction requires us to hold the good and the bad in tension with one another, rather than to play them off against each other. In other words, it requires evenhandedness and sympathy.

As an example, consider the relationship between the church and political power. One of my current areas of academic research is the Christianization of Scandinavia in the tenth and eleventh centuries. The common way of telling this story in the literature is that this process was *all* politics—all empire building and calculated power-grabbing.[3] Basically, a king wants to consolidate power. Becoming a Christian will do that because it will strengthen various alliances, remove enemies from power and replace them with Christians, and so forth. So, the king gets baptized. And then his subjects get baptized. And now you have a Christian nation.

My work in this has been to argue that this is not the whole story. I am working through a text from medieval historian Adam of Bremen to show how many waves of missionaries from places like Germany and England were going into Denmark, Sweden, and Norway for several centuries. Many of them were martyred in the cruelest ways, and it was very emotional for me to discover the bravery of these Christians who sailed up to preach to the Vikings, who were at that time in history extremely violent. I am arguing that their actions created conditions that influenced later political developments.

The temptation here can be to focus on one of these dynamics to the neglect of the other. One person says, "It was martyrs, not politics, that made the difference." That could be my temptation in trying to offer the corrective I am seeking to make. And another person says, "It was politics, not martyrs, that made the difference." But both instincts are too simple. The messy reality is: it was both. There was both courageous martyrdom *and* political power-grabbing. You have to hold the good and the bad in tension to be true to history.

Consider the early church's stance toward issues of social justice. On the one hand, we must come to terms with deep tragedy and failure in this area. Take perhaps the two greatest premodern Christian theologians, St. Augustine and Thomas Aquinas. I consider both to be theological father figures, and with Augustine, a kind of spiritual father as well. I often find myself seeking to

---

3. E.g., Fletcher, *Conversion of Europe*, 416.

defend them from critique coming from different angles—sometimes secular, sometimes conservative evangelical.

But I have to admit that their positions on social issues are often disappointing and occasionally disturbing. For example, unfortunately, these two great theologians maintained that men and women did not constitute the image of God equally, and they fleshed that out in all kinds of unwholesome and unedifying ways. And that had a huge influence, such that there is a lot of sexism in the premodern Christian tradition.[4]

Or consider their views on slavery. They maintained that the institution of slavery was the result of the fall, and they opposed its worst abuses and crimes (especially Augustine). But they also maintained that slavery had utility in the current state of the world, in maintaining social order. So, the institution of slavery as such should be tolerated as a kind of punishment on the world.[5] Now, their views are complicated, but I think that is a broadly fair summary. Someone might want to quibble over the details, but suffice it to say that we do not find in them, or in so much of the premodern Christian tradition they influenced, the kind of abolitionism we might hope or expect.

So the question comes up: should we consider these as father-like figures? Just as some of us might wonder: should we reconstruct Evangelicalism? Is it even *worth* it?

Here, as elsewhere, we find that evenhandedness and sympathy are repaid. There is more to the story. Just like in Scandinavian history, the martyrs are not as visible as the politics, so there are other voices in the Christian tradition that are not as visible that represent a different social posture. For example, in the Eastern tradition we find Gregory of Nyssa. Gregory's fourth homily during Lent in 379 AD has been regarded by some as the most scathing critique of slaveholding in all of antiquity.[6]

---

4. Aquinas, *Summa Theologica* 1, q. 92, art. 1, spoke of women as "defective and misbegotten," resulting from a kind of defect in male seed. (Regrettably, the passage is not more forgivable in context.) Augustine likewise held many other views most of us would find sexist today, such as the claim that, if it were not for the purpose of procreation, another man would have been a far more suitable companion to Adam in the Garden of Eden: "How much more agreeably, after all, for conviviality and conversation, would two male friends live together on equal terms than man and wife?" (*Literal Meaning of Genesis* 9.5.9). The influence of Augustine and Aquinas was such that it led to a widespread perception in premodern theology that men and women did not constitute the image of God equally (e.g., a common theme is that men constitute the image of God by themselves, while women only did so in coordination to men).

5. For a discussion of Augustine's views on slavery in *The City of God*, see Chambers, "Slavery and Domination," 13–28.

6. For discussion of Gregory's views in historical context, see Maxwell, *Slavery and the Catholic Church*, 32–33.

Gregory starts off the sermon by asking: can you even imagine the arrogance of one person thinking they can *own* another human being as property? Throughout the sermon, he builds an argument against slavery from natural law, the image of God, and human equality.[7] What made Gregory's sermon so prophetic for its time is that he was not merely saying, "It is injustice when you mistreat a slave." He is saying, "It is injustice to ever *have* a slave." He was not merely condemning the abuses; he was condemning the institution of slavery as such. And that was very rare in antiquity.

So here again the temptation could be for us to look at Augustine and Aquinas and say, "The premodern church failed to oppose slavery." Or, in the other direction, we could look at Gregory and say, "The early church led the charge in opposing slavery." Once again we see the need for even-handedness and sympathy, to hold the two in tension.

These are just two examples of many others that could be given. A more recent example would be the tragic capitulation of many churches to Nazi power in 1930s Germany. Yet we see God raising up voices of truth like Dietrich Bonhoeffer and Martin Niemöller. And again, it is easy to focus on just the bad, or just the good.

This is also true in the Bible. Think of the character David. One danger could be to say, "David sinned grievously against Uriah and Bathsheba; therefore, he was not really a man after God's own heart." Another danger would be to say, "David was a man after God's own heart; therefore, he did not really sin that badly." The fact is that David was complicated.

What does this have to do with reconstructing Evangelicalism? The same dynamics play out in Evangelicalism today. There is a mixture of good and bad. And we have to hold the two in tension as we consider reconstruction. If we focus on the good to the neglect the bad, we end up minimizing evil. This is a serious problem. There are real problems and sins in American Evangelicalism. If we want to know how grievously wrong that is, just think about times in your life when you have been mistreated, and someone comes along and says, "It was not that bad!" When Christians minimize evils in the church, it damages the very reputation of God.

On the other hand, if we focus on the bad to the neglect of the good, we end up rejecting or marginalizing the work of the Holy Spirit. It often strikes me that the context for Jesus's warning against blasphemy of the Holy Spirit in Matt 12 is rebuking the Pharisees for failing to recognize an exorcism. He is saying, in effect, "Satan does not cast out demons, so you should recognize this as the work of God."[8] So also today, we do not want to fail to discern

---

7. For a representative passage, see Maxwell, *Slavery and the Catholic Church*, 33.

8. "But if it is by the Spirit of God that I cast out demons, then the kingdom of God has come upon you" (Matt 12:28 ESV).

the genuine work of the Holy Spirit, wherever it is found. Therefore we need evenhandedness and sympathy to recognize both the good and bad in Evangelicalism, just as we must do with prior church history.

Now let me address three objections before we move on. First, some might worry that this call for evenhandedness and sympathy leads to compromise. For example, it might cause us to minimize or rationalize evil. I want to acknowledge that this is a legitimate concern. People had this concern with Obama's attitude toward Rev. Wright. And Obama did eventually distance himself more fully from Wright.

So let us make a crucial distinction here. We are not saying, "in Evangelicalism there is both good and bad; therefore adopt a neutral posture toward the whole." Rather, we are saying, "in Evangelicalism there is both good and bad; therefore distinguish between the two, so that we can be 100 percent *for* the good, and 100 percent *against* the bad." In other words, evenhandedness and sympathy does not mean *downplaying* the bad in relation to the good, but *distinguishing* the bad from the good. Therefore, done rightly, this posture is not compromise. It is simply accuracy.

This also answers a second objection that comes from the other direction: namely, that openly acknowledging the bad in church history means we are slandering the church. This is a concern that can be discerned from some quarters. If you speak out against sins in the church, you will have people telling you are slandering the church; you are smearing the reputation of Christ's bride, and so forth. But slander involves false accusation; the goal of evenhandedness and sympathy is truth, and the truth is, there *is* sin and dysfunction in the church. And we acknowledge those sins because we love the church and desire to see her healed from them.

Here's a third objection. Some say, "There is not *always* a mixture of good and bad in every circumstance. Sometimes it is just bad!" And this is true. There are many particular situations that are so toxic and so abusive that even evenhandedness and sympathy are not appropriate responses. However, this tends to be the case when you are focusing on a more specific, targeted reality—like one church or maybe even one region or tradition. But Evangelicalism has around 500 million people, and it is exploding in the global South; therefore, evenhandedness and sympathy get really important to the extent that you are talking about a large, diverse phenomenon.

Now the point we have made thus far is fairly simple, but I believe it is important to remember right now amidst the polarization that pressures us toward more totalizing judgments. And that basic point now sets us up for the larger and more complicated question of the goal of reconstruction.

PART TWO: OPPORTUNITIES

The Goal of Reconstruction

What should be reconstructed? In other words, if there is both good and bad within Evangelicalism, how do we know what the good is to support, and the bad is to reject?

Once again, church history can help us. Although for Protestants tradition is not infallible rule, it is a powerful testimony that can help us disentangle the wheat from the chaff and reenvision orthodoxy for a new day. For example, it can provide a non-Western perspective and a premodern perspective.

To make this point, let me share my own story of deconstruction. I grew up in a Christian home, and I have never rejected faith. But I have been through two seasons of great angst in my faith. Both involved fairly substantive deconstruction. The first was in college. The second one was over the last six or so years. As far as I can tell, the cause for this more recent season of angst was twofold: first, intellectual shifts related to questions of science (like evolution and climate change). Second, disillusionment about the current political and cultural dynamics within many circles of American Evangelicalism.

During this process, I found tremendous refuge in apologetics. My process of reconstruction involved landing back more solidly in two foundational bedrock convictions: the existence of God and the resurrection of Christ. I came to feel more deeply that a naturalistic worldview is more arbitrary, less interesting, less plausible, and ultimately dehumanizing. I develop this thesis in my book *Why God Makes Sense in a World That Doesn't*.[9] So there was a kind of reconstruction or landing more solidly back into Christianity.

I also landed back more firmly in Protestantism. That is the main focus of my YouTube ministry, "Truth Unites." I also did not become either a full-blown liberal or fundamentalist. So in this basic theological sense, I am still an Evangelical. At the same time, I also have become more open to consider what needs to be disentangled from a healthy evangelical faith in terms of the political, cultural, social, and doctrinal expressions of that in our context over recent decades. And I have not figured that all out.

What does this have to do with church history? What helped me most in wrestling with the question of evolution is St. Augustine. Reading St. Augustine's struggle through the book of Genesis was like oxygen. Many Evangelicals have the idea that a literalistic reading of Genesis is the default conservative view—and then in the modern era, because of the pressures of modern science, Christians had to adjust. But Augustine affirmed animal death before the fall. He was very patient at harmonizing Scripture and what we call "science," and he was quite happy to interpret not only Genesis 1, but to some degree,

---

9. Ortlund, *Why God Makes Sense*.

Genesis 2–3, in a nonliteral, nonwooden manner. But most of all, his whole posture to those questions—and the humility of his posture—created breathing room to struggle through those questions.[10]

This is an example of one way that church history can induce even-handedness and sympathy in evaluating the goal of reconstruction: it helps us reassess what is really central. Where have we drawn the boundaries in the wrong place? Evangelicalism has certain eccentricities; there are doctrines we assume as the normal or safe view that are actually either rare or controversial, or both, throughout church history. Another example of this would be the doctrine of last things, or eschatology. Many evangelical Christians assume dispensational premillennialism as a kind of default. But the very view that seems normal and default to us is the historical outlier. If you could take the *Left Behind* series and send it back in a time machine to the early church, the church fathers would be utterly mystified.

In an area like this, church history can help broaden us in ways we have gotten too narrow. In a process of deconstruction and reconstruction, you will come out on the other end more open-minded. However, it can also work the other way. Church history can also reveal things we undervalue, have forgotten, neglected, or define too broadly. An example in this direction would be the sacraments. One way that Evangelicalism tends to be different from all prior church history is in having a lower view of the sacraments and a lower ecclesiology overall. Church history would encourage us to consider that our worship services should have less of an entertainment feel—and should instead reflect more liturgical depth, greater aesthetic sensitivity, and a richer sacramental theology and practice.

A more controversial example would be our understanding of sexuality, gender, and marriage. Some feel, for example, that in order to reconstruct Evangelicalism we should adopt a more inclusive posture toward gay marriage. The testimony of church history would not support this position. On the doctrine of creation or end times, we are noting *differences* between evangelical theology and classical, mainstream Christianity. But defining marriage as between one man and one woman is not an evangelical eccentricity. It is something Evangelicals largely share with the non-Western church, and with basically the entire premodern church—patristic, medieval, and early modern. So a change in an area like that would be less about reconstructing Evangelicalism and more about reconstructing Christianity wholesale.

Related to this, there are many criticisms of Evangelicalism for promoting a hypermasculine and sexist culture. As one who is open to consider where there is some truth to this, I also think these criticisms are often unfair

---

10. On these points, see my *Retrieving Augustine's Doctrine*.

to modern Evangelicals since they could apply equally or more so to the premodern Christian world. For example, the word "complementarianism" has come to be associated for some with abuse, patriarchy, prejudice, sexism, etc. But the basic idea that the higher office in the church of teaching and leadership (whether called priest or presbyter/bishop/elder) is restricted to men is characteristic of non-Western, nonwhite Evangelicalism even more than Western, white Evangelicalism. It is also characteristic of the Roman Catholic Church, the Eastern Orthodox Church, the Oriental Orthodox Church, and the Assyrian Church of the East. It is also characteristic of basically all premodern Christianity, to my awareness.

If we value the insights and perspectives of our non-Western, nonwhite, premodern, and non-Protestant brothers and sisters in the faith, this should induce caution. We must continually be open to considering where our critiques may be too influenced by modern, Western values. In the task of reconstruction, we must have great humility—fear and trembling before God. One factor that can help is to remember that our efforts at reconstruction will fall short in some way or another, and therefore succeeding generations will be doing deconstruction and reconstruction with what they inherit from us.

If we are to be faithful to Christ in the times in which we live, we must resist the pressures that direct us toward one extreme or the other. This means open acknowledgment of evil. But it also means open acknowledgment of *good*. It means the evenhandedness and sympathy that allows for *both* deconstruction and reconstruction. In my own time of deconstruction, I had dark moments. I had times where I could not see the pathway before me. What got me through was apologetics and church history because these were *reconstructive* forces in my heart and imagination. When we are going through deconstruction, we need the counterbalancing forces of reconstruction. As we live in the tension of those competing forces, and surrender to the Holy Spirit's work, being vulnerable to the point of extreme honesty, we will emerge on the other side with a stronger faith and witness.

Conclusion

Aleksandr Solzhenitsyn was a decorated soldier in the Russian army, but was imprisoned near the end of World War II for disparaging comments he made about Joseph Stalin. And it was there in the desolation of prison, looking back on his life, that he finally came to understand the subtle nature of the struggle between good and evil in the human heart and how poignant, delicate, and even deceptive is the interplay of good and evil within each human person:

In my most evil moments I was convinced that I was doing good, and I was well supplied with systematic arguments. And it was only when I lay there on rotting prison straw that I sensed within myself the first stirrings of good. Gradually it was disclosed to me that the line separating good and evil passes not through states, nor between classes, nor between political parties either—but right through every human heart—and through all human hearts. This line shifts. Inside us, it oscillates with the years. And even within hearts overwhelmed by evil, one small bridgehead of good is retained. And even in the best of all hearts, there remains ... an un-uprooted small corner of evil.[11]

Solzhenitsyn's comments remind us that this mixture of both good and bad we have been saying is in Evangelicalism, and church history, is also true of *every single one of us*.

This is why we need our identity in the gospel of Jesus Christ. And it is why we need evenhandedness and sympathy as we move forward as the church.

Bibliography

Aquinas, Thomas. *Summa Theologica*. Translated by Fathers of the English Dominican Province. Notre Dame, IN: Christian Classics, 1948.

Augustine. *The Literal Meaning of Genesis*. In *On Genesis*, edited by John Rotelle, translated by Edmund Hill, 155–506. Hyde Park, NY: New City, 2002.

Chambers, Katherine. "Slavery and Domination as Political Ideas in Augustine's City of God." *Heythrop Journal* 54.1 (2013) 13–28.

Fletcher, Richard. *Conversion of Europe: From Paganism to Christianity, 371–1386 AD*. London: Fontana, 1998.

Hosking, Geoffrey A. *Beyond Socialist Realism: Soviet Fiction Since Ivan Denisovich*. New York: Holmes & Meier, 1980.

Maxwell, John Francis. *Slavery and the Catholic Church: The History of Catholic Teaching Concerning the Moral Legitimacy of the Institution of Slavery*. London: Barry Rose, 1975.

Obama, Barack. *A Promised Land*. New York: Crown, 2020.

———. "A More Perfect Union." Address at the National Constitution Center, Philadelphia, Pennsylvania, March 18, 2008. The American Presidency Project. https://www.presidency.ucsb.edu/node/277610.

Ortlund, Gavin. *Retrieving Augustine's Doctrine of Creation: Ancient Wisdom for Current Controversy*. Downers Grove, IL: IVP Academic, 2020.

———. *Why God Makes Sense in a World That Doesn't: The Beauty of Christian Theism*. Grand Rapids: Baker, 2021.

---

11. As cited in Hosking, *Beyond Socialist Realism*, 120.

10

The End of the Gospel

Refocusing Our "Why" as a Wesleyan Contribution to Reconstructing Evangelicalism

MATT O'REILLY

INTRODUCTION: THE CHALLENGE OF RECONSTRUCTING EVANGELICALISM

THE DIFFICULTIES THAT WILL come with reconstructing Evangelicalism should not be lost on any who set themselves to the task. Serious questions have been raised regarding quarters of Evangelicalism that supported racism in general and slavery in particular. Political entanglement has at times undermined evangelical credibility. Public scandal and the revelation of cases of abuse have caused some to ask whether Evangelicalism should be reconstructed at all. Another prominent challenge to reconstructing Evangelicalism comes with its vast multiplicity. There is no evangelical denomination, no formal structure, no constitution, no universally binding body of doctrine. The movement is often identified by certain leaders or institutions. But no single person or institution defines the movement. Evangelicals are present in any number of denominations. We could find evangelical Baptists and evangelical Methodists. There are evangelical Presbyterians and evangelical Lutherans. Not to mention the many denominations associated with the charismatic movement or those who would identify as Evangelicals within the Anglican Communion. The problem is even further complicated when "evangelical" is seen as a political category rather than a theological one. Indeed, one historian has remarked, "when viewed from the perspective of our multiplicity, we Evangelicals hold hardly anything in common."[1] To emphasize the difficulty, Alister McGrath reports that in 1986 Gallup and other pollsters gave up their attempts to discern a consistent set of evangelical beliefs. They opted instead to gauge self-identification by asking: "Would you describe yourself as a born-again Christian?"[2] The problem of clearly defining Evangelicalism crops up again and again, which frames the difficulty of our task. How are we to reconstruct something so difficult to define?

Nevertheless, historians argue that despite its varied expressions, Evangelicalism remains a "definite and definable" movement.[3] Perhaps the most well-known attempt to define the movement came in the form of Bebbington's evangelical quadrilateral. In 1989, he argued that Evangelicals are united by a focus on conversionism, activism, biblicism, and crucicentrism.[4] These four characteristics have stood for more than thirty years as standard evangelical commitments. In 1995, McGrath argued that Evangelicalism is built on what he calls "six controlling convictions."

1. The supreme authority of Scripture as a source of knowledge of God and a guide to Christian living.

2. The majesty of Jesus Christ, both as incarnate God and Lord and as the Savior of sinful humanity.

3. The lordship of the Holy Spirit.

4. The need for personal conversion.

5. The priority of evangelism for both individual Christians and the church as a whole.

6. The importance of the Christian community for spiritual nourishment, fellowship, and growth.[5]

It is no surprise that McGrath's "controlling convictions" overlap to some degree with Bebbington's "evangelical characteristics." And we can appreciate McGrath's attempt to strengthen the definition with a more robust trinitarianism and attention to the importance of discipleship. He frames Evangelicalism

---

1. Sweeney, *American Evangelical Story*, 20.

2. McGrath, *Evangelicalism*, 53. For a survey of the historical development of the term "evangelical" see, Noll, *Rise of Evangelicalism*, 16–21.

3. Sweeney, *American Evangelical Story*, 23.

4. Bebbington, *Evangelicalism in Modern Britain*.

5. McGrath, *Evangelicalism*, 55–56.

not only in terms of doctrinal commitments but also of devotional ethos; it is a movement in which knowledge of God is not mere abstraction but "capable of transforming both the heart and mind."[6]

Rather than attempting to identify distinguishing features of Evangelicals, Douglas Sweeney defines the movement in terms of its historical influences: "Evangelicals comprise a movement that is rooted in classical Christian orthodoxy, shaped by a largely Protestant understanding of the gospel, and distinguished from other such movements by an eighteenth-century twist."[7] By an eighteenth-century twist, Sweeney means that Evangelicals are defined by practices that grew out of the Great Awakening.[8] Sweeney understands Evangelicalism as a coalition (in contrast to a denomination or church) of Christians who work together to achieve a shared goal, namely "gospel witness."[9] As a coalition, participants self-select on a voluntary basis, and there is no way to be excommunicated, since no formal rules govern adherents.[10] Participants in this movement hold to theological convictions most clearly set forth in the Protestant Reformation and set within a broad Christian orthodoxy. Most important for our purposes is Sweeney's argument that Evangelicalism "emerged from a very definite, *eighteenth-century* cultural context, one that yielded a *twist* on Protestant orthodoxy."[11] That is to say that modern Evangelicals stand downstream from the revivals of the Great Awakening. Taking a cue from Sweeney's focus on Evangelicalism's legacy, we will shortly return to one eighteenth-century Evangelical in particular as we consider strategies for reconstructing the movement today.

Before proceeding with a constructive vision for the future of Evangelicalism, we do well to orient ourselves to the subgroups within the movement. The above definitions help us with the *what* of Evangelicalism, but what about the *who*? Drawing on Gabriel Fackre, Alister McGrath described the diversity of Evangelicalism in 1995 by listing six subgroups within the larger movement.

1. Fundamentalists, for whom "ultra-inerrancy" is a litmus test of faithfulness.

2. Old Evangelicals, who prioritize the experiential side of faith as the experience of regeneration.

3. New Evangelicals, who emphasize the apologetics and social importance of the faith.

---

6. McGrath, *Evangelicalism*, 57.
7. Sweeney, *American Evangelical Story*, 23–24.
8. Sweeney, *American Evangelical Story*, 24.
9. Sweeney, *American Evangelical Story*, 24.
10. Sweeney, *American Evangelical Story*, 24.
11. Sweeney, *American Evangelical Story*, 25 (emphasis original).

4. Justice and peace Evangelicals, who are committed to activism and a political agenda that stands in contrast to the religious right.

5. Charismatic Evangelicals, who focus on manifestations of the Spirit like speaking in tongues and supernatural healing.

6. Ecumenical Evangelicals, who desire to relate the movement to the broader Christian community.[12]

While these categories may resonate with those familiar with the history of Evangelicalism, the movement has changed in the years since that list was compiled. Rather than speaking of six "varieties of Evangelicalism" as McGrath did, Michael Graham has argued that we should recognize a six-way "fracturing of Evangelicalism." According to Graham, "Evangelicalism seems to be fracturing into at least 6 different subgroups. Three of those groups (#s 1–3) still have at least some connectivity to Evangelicalism and the other three have cut ties (#s 4–6)."[13]

1. Neo-Fundamentalists are deeply concerned about political and theological liberalism and with the church's drift toward secularism.

2. Mainstream Evangelicals tend to identify with Bebbington's quadrilateral and emphasize the Great Commission. They are worried about the influence of secular right politics on the church but are even more concerned with the influence of the secular left.

3. Neo-Evangelicals hold to typical evangelical doctrines but are less likely to use the term "evangelical" because its meaning has become far less clear, especially given that the term is often more associated with politics than theology.

4. Post-Evangelicals are those who have formally left the movement but still affirm the historic Christian creeds. They tend to be vocally critical of 1s and 2s. Some are still Protestant, but others have moved to mainline denominations, Roman Catholicism, or Orthodoxy.

5. Dechurched (but with some Jesus) have left the church but still hold some Christian beliefs.

6. Dechurched and deconverted have left the church and no longer identify with Christianity at all.

These categories should not be taken as altogether fixed and firm. For Graham, some people exist in between two of the above categories. The most significant

12. McGrath, *Evangelicalism*, 107–8.
13. Graham, "Six Way Fracturing," para. 8.

fault lines are 1s vs. 3s and 2s vs. 4s. Group 1 and group 4 have largely stopped worshipping together. While a full analysis of this taxonomy is beyond the scope of this work, it does helpfully illustrate both the difficulty with reconstructing Evangelicalism and the need to reconstruct Evangelicalism. Not only are we dealing with a variety of approaches to defining the movement, we also have a range of different social groups both within the movement and in relation to it, some of which are deeply, deeply critical of some others. The likelihood of casting a vision of the future of the movement that will satisfy all parties is slim (and that itself may be an overstatement). Nevertheless, we are positioned to consider a vision that might inspire those who remain committed in some degree to the vision of Evangelicalism. For that, we turn now to one eighteenth-century figure whose evangelical commitments helped spark revivals on two continents and heavily influenced the rise of modern Evangelicalism.[14] That figure is John Wesley. More specifically, we will turn to his understanding of *why* God was at work amid the movement that came to bear his name.

The "Why" of Eighteenth-Century Methodism

John Wesley regularly gathered the early Methodist preachers to confer on their shared mission and ministry. The records of their conferences often took the form of questions and answers, and on one occasion they raised the *why* question.[15] I am sure you are familiar with the *why* question. You have likely asked it yourself at least once or twice, and you likely know that it can take slightly different forms. Why does God have us here? Why does God have us doing this? What is the reason for our ministry? What are God's purposes in our work? Wesley and his preachers framed the question this way: "What may we reasonably believe to be God's design in raising up the Preachers called Methodists?"[16] They recorded their answer this way: "Not to form any new sect; but to reform the nation, particularly the Church; and to spread scriptural holiness over the land."[17] When the *why* question was raised, this group of early Evangelicals answered by highlighting their conviction that God had raised them up to "spread scriptural holiness." This was their reason for being, their motivation, their mission. Their commitment to holiness shaped their self-understanding, and it shaped their movement. And their movement is

---

14. Cf. Sweeney, *American Evangelical Story*, 36–42.
15. Cf. O'Reilly, "New Testament Vision," 91.
16. Wesley, *Works*, 8:299.
17. Wesley, *Works*, 8:299.

a critical part of the evangelical story. For Wesley, holiness was the *telos* of the Christian religion in general and the Christian gospel in particular. But despite Wesley's influence on the emergence and growth of Evangelicalism, his commitment to cultivating holiness did not become a defining feature of modern Evangelicalism. That brings me to the central exhortation of this essay. If we are going to reconstruct Evangelicalism, we should do so with a view to the *telos* of the Christian faith in general and of the gospel in particular. And we can take our cue from the way Wesley and the people called Methodists answered the *why* question. To put it another way, Evangelicals *ought* to make the end of the gospel the *why* of Evangelicalism. We do that by recovering Wesley's commitment to the spread of scriptural holiness.

This exhortation will proceed in two further steps. First, we will take a look at Wesley's sermon, "The Scripture Way of Salvation." This sermon will prove useful because Wesley explicitly articulates his understanding of the end (or *telos*) of the Christian faith. We will note along the way how his understanding differs from the customary ways Evangelicalism has come to be defined as we have outlined them above, but we will also consider the way his vision resonates with the inclinations of modern Evangelicalism. Second, we will turn to Paul's letter to the Romans (a favorite among so many Evangelicals) as a test case in considering whether Wesley's vision of the end of religion (and the gospel) stands up to scriptural rigor.

Wesley and the End of Religion

Wesley's sermon, "The Scripture Way of Salvation," is his account of the language of "salvation" and "faith" as they are used in Eph 2:8. He begins by contrasting the complexity and difficulty of heathen religions with the simplicity of "the genuine religion of Jesus Christ; provided that we take it in its native form, just as it is described in the oracles of God!"[18] He proceeds to celebrate God's gracious wisdom in revealing that genuine religion to us given our present state of fallenness. This clarity and accessibility is observable, Wesley says, "both with regard to the end it proposes, and the means to attain that end!"[19] He then states explicitly, "The end is, in one word, salvation; the means to attain it, faith."[20] For Wesley, those two words—salvation and faith—"include the substance of all the Bible, the marrow, as it were, of the whole Scripture."[21]

---

18. Wesley, *Works*, 6:43.

19. Wesley, *Works*, 6:43. Collins notes that Wesley came to see holiness as the end of religion as early as 1725; see Collins, *John Wesley*, 35.

20. Wesley, *Works*, 6:43.

21. Wesley, *Works*, 6:44.

In light of these considerations, the sermon proceeds with three questions: (1) What is salvation? (2) What is that faith whereby we are saved? And (3) how are we saved by it?[22]

The meaning of "salvation" in the context of Eph 2:8 is crucial for Wesley's understanding of the *telos* of the Christian faith. Salvation, for him, is not mere conversion. That is crucial, but it is insufficient as a synonym for salvation. Neither does Wesley see this reference in Eph 2:8 as having to do with future post-mortem salvation, whether that is understood as heaven, entrance into paradise, or eternal happiness. For Wesley, the salvation spoken of in Eph 2:8 is not distant but present, a blessing of which believers are *now* in possession. That present work is certainly built on the gracious "drawings of the Father" and extends to all the future saving works of God until they are "consummated in glory."[23] But in Wesley's view, those works are not in view in this text.

What does the apostle here mean with his language of salvation? Wesley says it "consists of two general parts, justification and sanctification."[24] Wesley sees justification primarily as a forensic term involving pardon or forgiveness and acceptance by God. The basis of our justification "is the blood and righteousness of Christ; or . . . all that Christ hath done and suffered for us."[25] Wesley includes a parenthetical note that this is "commonly termed the meritorious cause of our justification."[26] Simultaneous with our justification is the experience of the new birth, which involves a real change, an inward renewal which is the result of the power of God. This involves an immediate experience of the love of God and produces love for others and expels the love of the world, pleasure, ease, honor, money, pride, anger, self-will, and other evil postures (or "tempers" as Wesley called them). He notes that new believers may easily be deceived into thinking that all sin is gone from them at this time. However, he continues, they quickly find they are mistaken when "temptations return, and sin revives; showing it was but stunned before, not dead."[27] This experience brings Wesley to the importance of sanctification as a component of salvation.

---

22. Wesley, *Works*, 6:44.

23. Wesley, *Works*, 6:44. For an extended discussion of prevenient (or preventing) grace, see Shelton, *Prevenient Grace*.

24. Wesley, *Works*, 6:44.

25. Wesley, *Works*, 6:45.

26. Wesley, *Works*, 6:45. For Wesley's extended discussion and affirmation of the active and passive righteousness of Christ imputed to the believer, see his sermon "The Lord our Righteousness," in *Works*, 5:234–46.

27. Wesley, *Works*, 6:45.

Now Wesley's view of sanctification has been the object of plenty of criticism. But I invite you to lend a charitable ear to this account, remembering that Wesley stood firmly convinced that God raised up the Methodist movement for the express purpose of preaching this doctrine, this experience. He was deeply convicted that this doctrine of holiness is a biblical doctrine—thus his language of "scriptural holiness." It is important to know that he regularly used the language of "entire sanctification" and "full salvation" and "Christian perfection" interchangeably, a practice he employs in "The Scripture Way of Salvation." But how does Wesley understand this crucial doctrine around which early evangelical Methodism was organized and which formed its *telos*?

Wesley exhorted new believers to mortify sin and set themselves to good works. Neither of these efforts should be understood in any meritorious sense. To the contrary, both, for Wesley, are enabled by the Holy Spirit. The believer's posture is to do good works—works of piety and mercy—while he or she *waits* for entire sanctification. A posture of waiting highlights the way Wesley sees entire sanctification as a gift of grace. The believer cannot produce nor accomplish entire sanctification. Only the Spirit can do that. Works of piety and works of mercy function as a means of grace through which Christ is formed in the believer and through which the Holy Spirit will do the work of entire sanctification. So, Wesley says, "It is thus that we wait for the entire sanctification; for a full salvation from all our sins—from pride, self-will, anger, unbelief; or, as the apostle expresses it, 'go on unto perfection.' But what is perfection?" he asks. "It is love excluding sin; love filling the heart, taking up the whole capacity of the soul. It is love 'rejoicing evermore, praying without ceasing, in everything giving thanks.'"[28] If the language of "waiting" as an indication of the gracious nature of entire sanctification is the first thing we note about Wesley's doctrine of holiness, the second is the language of "perfect love." A crucial feature of Wesley's understanding of sanctification is that holiness is not exclusively the negation of sin. Mortification is not enough. This is because, for Wesley, while sin is the violation of divine law, it is not merely that. Sin represents a ruptured relationship between us and the triune God. So even if a believer could successfully do away with all sin, it would not, in Wesley's understanding, constitute entire sanctification. Rather, he draws our attention to the importance of God's perfect love poured into our hearts. Entire sanctification is this positive experience of perfect love from Father, Son, and Holy Spirit to us. Upon that experience of perfect love, the believer's desires are thoroughly reoriented, by grace, toward God. The believer is filled with love for God and neighbor. And that love, having filled the heart, leaves no quarter for sin. Sin is excluded by perfect love. To sum up, Wesleyan entire

---

28. Wesley, *Works*, 6:46.

sanctification is not the mortification of sin until one manages to get rid of it all; rather, entire sanctification (holiness!) is an experience of divine love that is so complete and thorough and comprehensive that sin is driven out of the believer's heart with no room left for it because our whole self is occupied by perfect love.

Wesley was committed to the language of "perfection" because he found that language in the Bible.[29] And he desired to be "a man of one book." If the language of perfection and entire sanctification is in the Scripture, Wesley reasoned, then its use is warranted, and a hesitancy to employ that language might say more about one's posture toward the Bible than one's posture toward Wesley. Nevertheless, Wesley was careful to offer a nuanced account of "perfection" language in the Bible. He insisted in his sermon on "Christian Perfection" and in his tract "Principles of a Methodist" that the term did not imply freedom from ignorance, freedom from mistake, freedom from infirmity (i.e., nonmoral imperfections), or freedom from temptation.[30] It did mean two things: freedom from willful and habitual sinful behaviors and freedom from evil thoughts; these having been excluded by an experience of perfect love.[31] Much more could be said (and has been said) about Wesley's doctrine of holiness.[32] I hope these contours will suffice to start our conversation with regard to how the *why* of early evangelical Methodism might help us refocus any effort to reconstruct the larger movement in the present day. At this point, the listener might respond by saying: that is all well and good, but should we not ask that crucial question that every good Evangelical is taught to always ask: Is it biblical? Does Wesley's account of entire sanctification stand up to scriptural rigor? For those questions, we will turn to a book of the Bible prized and beloved by so many in the evangelical movement.

The Question of Holiness in the Letter to the Romans

It may seem counterintuitive to some to consider the question of holiness in Romans. After all, the majority of scholarship on Paul's longest and most influential letter has focused on the doctrine of justification with much less

---

29. E.g., Matt 5:48; Phil 3:15; cf. 1 Thess 5:23.

30. For "Christian Perfection," see Wesley, *Works*, 6:1–22; for "Principles of a Methodist," see Wesley, *Works*, 8:361–74.

31. Wesley, *Works*, 6:6, 16.

32. The terms "holiness," "Christian perfection," and "entire sanctification" are often used interchangeably in the study of Wesley's theology. For Wesley's vision of holiness see, "Christian Perfection," *Works*, 6:1–22; cf., Lindström, *Wesley and Sanctification*; Collins, *Theology of John Wesley*, 279–312; Watson, *Perfect Love*.

attention being given to holiness and sanctification. Nevertheless, there is good reason to look to this letter, if only because Paul raises what I have elsewhere called "the question of holiness," even if the question is put negatively.[33] "Should we continue in sin in order that grace may abound?" (Rom 6:1; cf. 6:15 NRSV). The apostle's answer to that question would likely surprise any Evangelical who had been taught that the process of sanctification was more like sin management than an experience of divine love wrought by the Holy Spirit that frees us from sin (Rom 5:5; 6:18). But does Paul's vision of holiness resonate with Wesley's account? Our reflections on that question turn on five points.

First, in Romans the language of salvation is used in the comprehensive way that characterized Wesley's thought. That language does not, we should note, refer minimally to the moment of conversion, justification, or regeneration, as it is commonly used in North American Evangelicalism. Romans 1:16–17 sets forth Paul's theological agenda for the whole letter. He will articulate his gospel because it is the way God gives salvation to both Jew and Gentile. It is the way God reveals and defends his righteous character. The rest of the letter opens up and fills in what is meant by the term "salvation" in 1:16. This includes Paul's account of justification in Rom 3:21—4:25. The language of salvation also includes his account of sanctification set forth in 6:1—8:17 and even extends to future bodily resurrection in 8:18–25 (especially 8:23). It should not be controversial that Wesley's comprehensive understanding of salvation language is unquestionably Pauline and deeply biblical in shape.

Second, even though justification has been the focus of so much work in Romans, justification is not for Paul a *telos* in and of itself. Justification alone does not solve the problem of sin as it is articulated in 1:18—3:20. Rather, justification plays an instrumental role in the order of salvation. It is the means to the end of holiness. And only when believers embody the character of the triune God in holiness understood as perfect love do we have a sufficient solution to the problem of sin as it is articulated at the beginning of Romans. This is why the theme of life in the Spirit forms the climax of the first half of the letter. Holiness is where the argument of Romans is going all along.

Third, Paul's answer to the question of holiness does not sound like someone who says, "Well, I am only human. What else can I do but sin?" Paul gives no counsel for managing the ongoing problem of sin. He simply says, "Stop sinning!" That's the implication of 6:1, "Shall we continue in sin . . . ? By no means!" This exhortation is grounded in and deeply integrated with Paul's positive vision of union with Christ and life in the Spirit. It is grounded on the reality that God has poured his love into our hearts in order to thoroughly

---

33. O'Reilly, "'Shall We Continue in Sin?'"

change our character. Wesley built his doctrine of holiness around the logic of Romans, and he took salvation understood as climaxing in holiness as the *telos* of the Christian faith because that is the shape it takes in Scripture generally and in Romans particularly.

Fourth, the larger structure of Romans bears this out. The entire document is framed with the literary structure of *inclusio*. That is, it begins and ends with the same theme. Paul introduces himself as the apostle called to produce obedience from the nations (1:5). He ends the letter by repeating this vocation twice. In 15:18, he "will not venture to speak of anything except what Christ has accomplished through me to *win obedience from the Gentiles*" (emphasis added). In the doxology of 16:26 he celebrates the command of God "to bring about the obedience of faith" among the nations. The principle of *inclusio* tells us that when we find the same theme both at the beginning and the end of a particular text, then everything in between should be interpreted in light of that bookending theme. Taken that way, Paul's vocation to procure obedience to Christ from the nations should govern the way we read everything in Romans, from the doctrine of sin to the doctrine of justification, from the doctrine of holiness to the question of table fellowship. Paul's ministry is motivated by a vision of the nations embodying the character of God revealed in Christ empowered by the Spirit. The apostle is after nothing less than global holiness. At the risk of anachronism, we could say that Paul's aim was to *spread scriptural holiness across the land*.

Fifth, this hermeneutic of holiness helps us with the major subunits that are Rom 9–11 and 12–15. In chapters 9–11, Paul himself takes up a posture of other-oriented holy love toward his kinsmen in the flesh. This is embodied in his willingness (perhaps even his eagerness) to be cut off from Christ for their sake, if only it would accomplish their reconciliation. Talk about perfect love. Is there any division in his heart? Is anything held back? Has not the love of God filled him so fully that self-interest has been excluded? And then in 12:1—15:13, we find the particular ethics that will characterize the Roman church when they are consumed with love for God and neighbor. The community is to be marked by love (12:9) and embody the character of Christ (15:7).

Much more could be said but space constrains us. Nevertheless, I hope these five brief points regarding the interpretation of Romans offer us two invitations. First, to see the way a hermeneutic of holiness has potential to make sense of the overall structure of Romans and the way each part relates to the others. Second, to see that Wesley's vision of holiness (and that of early evangelical Methodism) is deeply in tune with the document that has influenced Evangelicalism as much as any.

Conclusion: A Wesleyan Contribution to Reconstructing Evangelicalism

Early evangelical Methodists constructed a movement around the conviction that everyone could experience the love of God shed abroad in their hearts to such an extent that sin could be pushed out. They believed that regardless of one's particular sin or social status, the gracious work of God's perfect love is able to sanctify us through and through. This conviction regarding full salvation was a *telos* of their movement, and it moved them to ministry with every sort of person on the margins of society in eighteenth-century England and North America. They were compelled by the love of God and their scripturally grounded belief that *that* love could transform any person by grace through faith. And if you were to ask one of those early evangelical Methodists: Why Methodism? They would surely answer: Because holiness! This focus—this *telos*—of early evangelical Methodism cultivated its vitality and made it an integral part of the rise of modern Evangelicalism. Yet this distinctive conviction of early evangelical Wesleyans has not come to be distinctive of modern Evangelicalism. Yes, there is certainly a focus on conversionism and subsequent discipleship. But I fear Evangelicals may have, in general, made an end of that which Scripture frames as a means. Could it be that Evangelicalism has made conversion an end in itself rather than a means to the end of holy love filling the heart? If so, then the evangelical Wesleyan tradition has something to contribute to the reconstruction of the larger evangelical movement, and the evangelical Wesleyan tradition invites that larger evangelical movement to re-member and refocus on the goal of the *evangel*. If that led to the construction of a vital evangelical Methodism in the eighteenth century, perhaps it could contribute to the reconstruction of a healthier Evangelicalism today. Wesley recognized the need of his nation—indeed, of the world—to experience the comprehensive nature of God's perfect love. And he recognized the biblical resources to cultivate that transformative experience. Christ died to justify the ungodly not as an end but *as a means to the end* of making the ungodly holy. Is that not what it means to be a gospel people? And if so, should that not be what it means to be Evangelical?

Bibliography

Bebbington, David W. *Evangelicalism in Modern Britain: A History from the 1730s to the 1980s.* London: Routledge, 1989.

Collins, Kenneth J. *John Wesley: A Theological Journey.* Nashville: Abingdon, 2003.

———. *The Theology of John Wesley: Holy Love and the Shape of Grace.* Nashville: Abingdon, 2007.

Graham, Michael. "The Six Way Fracturing of Evangelicalism." *Mere Orthodoxy*, July 7, 2021. https://mereorthodoxy.com/six-way-fracturing-Evangelicalism/.

Lindström, Harold. *Wesley and Sanctification: A Study in the Doctrine of Salvation*. Nappanee, IN: Francis Asbury, 1980.

McGrath, Alister. *Evangelicalism and the Future of Christianity*. Downers Grove, IL: IVP, 1995.

Noll, Mark. *The Rise of Evangelicalism: The Age of Edwards, Whitefield and the Wesleys*. Downers Grove, IL: IVP, 2003.

O'Reilly, Matt. "A New Testament Vision for the Future of Global Methodism." In *The Next Methodism: Theological, Social, and Missional Foundations for Global Methodism*, edited by Kenneth J. Collins and Ryan N. Danker, 91–98. Franklin, TN: Seedbed, 2022.

———. "'Shall We Continue in Sin?' Human Flourishing and the Question of Holiness in Romans 6." *WTJ* 55.2 (2020) 102–13.

Shelton, W. Brian. *Prevenient Grace: God's Provision for Fallen Humanity*. Anderson, IN: Francis Asbury, 2014.

Sweeney, Douglas A. *The American Evangelical Story: A History of the Movement*. Grand Rapids: Baker, 2005.

Watson, Kevin M. *Perfect Love: Recovering Entire Sanctification—the Lost Power of the Methodist Movement*. Franklin, TN: Seedbed, 2021.

Wesley, John. *A Plain Account of Christian Perfection*. Franklin, TN: Seedbed, 2014.

———. *The Works of John Wesley*. Edited by Thomas Jackson, 14 vols. Grand Rapids: Baker, 2007.

11

Reconstructing an Architecture for Evangelical Cultural Interaction

WALTER KIM

INTRODUCTION

HE WAS THE TENNIS version of Yoda—short, old, wrinkled, but strong with the force. My tennis coach in high school was an elderly man with arthritis in his knees and shoulders. But whenever he stood on the court to run me through drills, the emphasis was indeed on me running. He knew every angle and spin possible; he knew where to hit the ball, so that I would dash frenetically around the court only to return the ball exactly back to him. This is when the difference between playing tennis and being a tennis player became apparent. The former may have verve; the latter had wisdom.

Evangelicals have been running around the court of culture, desperately trying to swat back the ideas coming at them. This whack-a-mole response to ideological threats (perceived or real) is frenetic, sometimes furious, and ultimately futile. Even more concerning for the honor and mission of Jesus are the ways in which Christians are contributing to making ideological whack-a-mole our national sport. We need a robust application of biblical faith for our common life in complex times. Of course, the gospel is powerfully countercultural. But does being countercultural require being pugnacious and

PART TWO: OPPORTUNITIES

pugilistic? Instead of the prevailing metaphor of culture war, in which we defend our position, attack our opponents, and seek to win ground, a generative metaphor of culture reconstruction would be more attuned to a Savior who "did not come to be served, but to serve, and to give his life as a ransom for many" (Mark 10:45). In looking for a new blueprint, we can turn to Solomon's temple, which reaches across the millennia and rouses our imagination for reconstructing Evangelicalism. The architecture of the temple and of Scripture itself exemplifies the nuanced interplay between the common grace manifest in general society and the special grace given to God's people.

More Than Home Improvement

The need to reconstruct Evangelicalism is more than a small home improvement project. Our country is experiencing a historic moment of transition. Those under eighteen years old constitute the first majority-minority generation in America. Our cultural mosaic is far more dynamic than ever before, with an infusion of experiences, values, perspectives, and traditions that has enriched but also complexified our national life. Simultaneously, there are gaping social wounds. Polarization is pulling us apart and clumping us into factions that are increasingly disconnected from and discontented with one another. And there are zip codes to our polarization. Subcultures exist between rural and urban America and between regions of the country that differ in accents and attitudes. Now, social media and geographical mobility have caused these differences to bump, and sometimes smash, into each other.

When we take a panoramic view of Western civilization, the challenges assume historic proportions. In *A Secular Age*, Charles Taylor compellingly argues that we are witnessing "a move from a society where belief in God is unchallenged, and indeed, unproblematic, to one in which it is understood to be one option among others, and frequently not the easiest one to embrace."[1] The intellectual historian Jacques Barzun contends that the West is in a period "full of deep concerns, but peculiarly restless, for it sees no clear lines of advance. The loss it faces is that of Possibility. The forms of art as of life seem exhausted, the stages of development have been run through. Institutions function painfully."[2] Thus, in the convergence of rapid social change and glacial forces unfolding over centuries, Evangelicalism is moving from the center to the margins of American society.

---

1. Taylor, *Secular Age*, 3.
2. Barzun, *From Dawn to Decadence*, xvi.

There are also centrifugal and centripetal forces deeply embedded within Evangelicalism. It is easier to get Evangelicals to sign a statement of faith than to agree on an approach to culture. In her work *Apostles of Reason*, historian Molly Worthen explores Evangelicalism's response to the challenges of modernity. She comments that "three elemental concerns unite [Evangelicals]: how to repair the fracture between spiritual and rational knowledge; how to assure salvation and a true relationship with God; and how to resolve the tension between the demands of personal belief and the constraints of a secularized public square."[3] When viewed through this conceptual framework, Evangelicalism is not only a set of theological principles but also a negotiation of cultural position and posture toward society.

The time-tested Bebbington Quadrilateral (conversionism, activism, biblicism, and crucicentrism)[4] captures unifying and defining beliefs about Scripture and salvation but does not specifically address how spiritual and secular knowledge relate or how Christians should operate in a pluralistic marketplace of ideas. While there are shared concerns, there are not shared conclusions. What holds together—or pushes apart—young earth creationists and evolutionary creationists, or Evangelicals who participated in Black Lives Matter marches and those who oppose CRT? We need better guiding principles to navigate these complexities.

Architecture of the Temple

Humans construct buildings, especially public ones, not simply for shelter but also for significance. The American architect Frank Lloyd Wright declared that "architecture is the scientific art of making structure express ideas."[5] The temple is God's unparalleled meaning-making structure. Throughout the Bible, it serves as the eschatological center of the cosmos at which the name of God would reside (Deut 12:5), to which the nations would stream (Isa 2:2–4), and from which the river of life would flow to heal the nations (Ezek 47). So fundamental was the temple to Israel's identity that the prophet Jeremiah rebuked the people for saying "this is the temple of the Lord!" as a mantra of divine approval (Jer 7:4 ESV). In the New Testament, Jesus uses the temple in a typological fashion when he says, "Destroy this temple and in three days I will raise it up again" (John 2:19 NET). With the destruction of Christ's body

---

3. Worthen, *Apostles of Reason*, 6.
4. Bebbington, *Evangelicalism in Modern Britain*, 2–19.
5. Gutheim, *Frank Lloyd Wright on Architecture*, 141.

as temple, as well as the destruction of Herod's temple, God's people became the new temple of God on earth (Eph 2:21; 1 Pet 2:5).

The temple's theological importance in the Bible arises in part because of the cultural importance of temples in antiquity. Since the ancient world was fundamentally religious, sacred buildings represented the "physical manifestations of the coming together of the creative and intellectual lives of the communities that built and used them."[6] In this context, the architecture of Solomon's temple displays an extraordinarily rich and nuanced interaction with the cultural milieu of the ancient Near East. Four things about the construction of the temple will help us with the reconstruction of Evangelicalism. First, the temple *received* and incorporated universal motifs expressive of the common human experience. Second, the temple *refined* and improved architectural practices of pagan temples. Third, although utilizing certain ideas from pagan cultures, the temple *rejected* hazardous ideologies. Lastly, the temple *reimagined* ancient architecture to communicate divine truth with extraordinary creativity.

Receive

A fundamental building block toward a biblical theology of cultural interaction recognizes that God's common grace endows humans with the curiosity and capacity to explore his creation. We all navigate life as embodied creatures, and our interactions with our surroundings come with powerfully subtle associations. In controlled experiments, psychologists noted that employers who reviewed résumés placed on a heavy clipboard judged those candidates to be more substantive than the same applications presented on light clipboards.[7] They were weightier in both the physical and metaphorical sense. Certain architectural motifs tap into these deep cognitive associations. Even today in Athens, the Parthenon's high perch over the city demands attention. When a tourist on the street looks up, the sky becomes the only background to the temple, and the line separating the heavens and the earth fades.

The biblical temple's location on Mt. Zion also employed this universal visual language of transcendence. As majestic as we might imagine Jerusalem to be, when Solomon ascended the throne, the town was merely fifteen or sixteen acres, or about a dozen football fields. The construction of the palace-temple precinct on the hilltop tripled the acreage of the city to about fifty acres.[8] The

---

6. Mierse, *Temples and Sanctuaries*, 228.
7. Ackerman, Nocera, and Bargh, "Incidental Haptic Sensations," 1712–15.
8. Tarler and Cahill, "David, City of," 65.

rapid transformation of the urban landscape gave the temple "the sense of awe and inspiration worthy of the dwelling of the national deity."[9] Because it was a physical GPS that dominated the skyline, the temple instinctively served as a theological GPS to command attention to Yahweh's kingship. Hence, ancient Israelites on pilgrimage to the temple would worship with songs of ascent like, "I lift up my eyes to the mountains—where does my help come from? My help comes from the Lord, the Maker of heaven and earth" (Ps 121:1–2 NIV).

Even more extraordinarily, the common grace of our embodied existence was coupled with a common effort. In the building of this temple, Solomon employed Hiram the king of Tyre, because the cedars of Lebanon and the skill of the Sidonians were unparalleled (1 Kgs 5:6). This means that the most sacred structure for God's people was built in collaboration with a pagan people, from whom God's people received insight and expertise.

Refine

In addition to receiving the gifts of common grace to achieve the purposes of God, Solomon refined prevailing practices, and so provides us with another building block of cultural interaction. The temple's tri-partite blueprint—portico, main room, and Most Holy Place (1 Kgs 6:3, 16–17)—matches the three-room designs of temples discovered at Ain Dara in Syria and at Tell Tayinat in Turkey.[10] This correspondence suggests an original pattern among the Phoenicians of Syria, which fits with the expected influence of Hiram of Tyre (noted above).[11] However, the biblical temple reveals an important development. Compared to the remains in Syria-Palestine, the biblical temple displayed a remarkable regard for mathematical proportionality, with the interior dimensions of twenty cubits wide, thirty cubits high, and sixty cubits long (1 Kgs 6:2), reflecting an arithmetic progression (1 Kgs 2:3, 6). Regarding the Parthenon (fifth century BCE), renowned architecture critic Sarah Goldhagen notes how "the complex interplay of embodied math and embodied physics creates a sense of rightness about the Parthenon's composition."[12] Centuries before the Athenians, Solomon's temple exhibited and recorded the spatial orientation and proportions of various rooms to embody the divine rightness of Yahweh's rule.

---

9. Cogan, *1 Kings*, 251.
10. Mazar, *Archaeology of the Land*, 377; King and Stager, *Life in Biblical Israel*, 334–38.
11. Cogan, *1 Kings*, 252.
12. Goldhagen, *Welcome to Your World*, 231.

PART TWO: OPPORTUNITIES

While the existence of meticulous architectural plans in the Bible may seem befuddling or perhaps boring to the modern reader, it should be a source of amazement and another building block toward a biblical theology of cultural interaction. Mesopotamian accounts of temples served typically as royal propaganda, but the extensive building narratives of the tabernacle (Exod 25–31; 35–40) and temple (1 Kgs 6–8; cf. Ezek 40–43) focused on the actual building and not the royal sponsor. The architectural blueprint and even mechanism of doorways (1 Kgs 6:34) "are striking in the exact details given ... the information provided by the biblical descriptions seems to be intent on enabling the reader actually to visualize the building or object described."[13] The uniqueness of the biblical account demonstrates that architecture became theology. Divine beauty and redemptive order, rather than royal propaganda, were underscored in this refinement of physical design and narrative recounting. There was an embrace of technology, engineering, art, and architecture not merely as neutral or ancillary endeavors but as essential means by which truth is communicated.

Reject

The third building block is the skillful extraction of ideas to be embraced from an overall ideology to be rejected. Until now, the focus has been on the structural architecture of the temple, but the biblical narrative includes extensive accounts of interior design and art. A typical visual language recurred throughout the ancient Near East. The *Investiture of Zimri-Lim*, a large mural discovered at the Royal Palace in the ancient Syrian city of Mari, depicts the king being coronated by the goddess Ishtar.[14] The broad scene contains two sacred trees with cherubim and flowers dispersed throughout the mural. The biblical temple incorporated these visual motifs in its design with wall carvings "in the form of gourds and open flowers" (1 Kgs 6:18 ESV), as well as "cherubim and palm trees and open flowers, in the inner and outer rooms" (1 Kgs 6:29 ESV). The design utilized common iconography, in which sacred trees, heavenly creatures, and luxuriant flora together signify a scenario of cosmic order and abundance.

Although the temple adopted some of this artistic language, it starkly repudiated other aspects to establish a powerful theological polemic: "When the Temple wall reliefs are compared to Mesopotamian examples, the most striking feature is the absence of the deity and the king from the Solomonic

---

13. Hurowitz, *I Have Built*, 245–46.
14. King and Stager, *Life in Biblical Israel*, 216.

depictions."[15] Throughout the ancient Near East the monarch typically served as the chief priest, and thereby concentrated religious and political authority in the throne. As opposed to the *Investiture of Zimri-Lim*, which centered the king's divine right to rule, Yahweh and Solomon were nowhere depicted visually in this fashion. Any subordination of religion to politics was roundly rejected. Indeed, when King Uzziah brashly entered the temple to burn incense on the altar, he was confronted by the priests and ultimately punished by God with disease (2 Chr 26:16–21).

Moreover, instead of the typical idol in the inner sanctuary, the Most Holy Place contained the ark of the covenant as the symbol of the covenantal relationship. Yahweh's royal presence was undoubtedly understood to be represented, as suggested by the formulaic epithet "the ark of the covenant of the Lord Almighty, who is enthroned between the cherubim" (1 Sam 4:4 NIV; cf. Pss 80:1; 99:1; Isa 37:16). The absence of a divine idol conveyed the theological commitments expressed in Solomon's dedicatory prayer that, on the one hand, "I have indeed built you an exalted house, a place for you to dwell in forever" (1 Kgs 8:13 ESV), but on the other hand, "Behold, heaven and the highest heaven cannot contain you; how much less this house that I have built!" (1 Kgs 8:27 ESV). The temple's interior design freely used common visual idioms of sacred order, even as it repudiated pagan royal indoctrination. This is not syncretism but God's revealed design.

Reimagine

Lastly, the temple reimagined how common human endeavors—art, architecture, engineering, collaboration—could be divinely inspired to reveal God and his mission in the world. The significance of the Most Holy Place was conveyed not only by its position buried deep within the structure or by its containment of the ark of the covenant, but also by its mathematical dimension as a perfect cube: 20 x 20 x 20 cubits. Once again, the extant examples of other temples in Syria-Palestine did not display such a concern for mathematical precision and proportion. Yet, from a design perspective that considers our embodied human perception, the cubic space would have produced a startling effect.

The shape of a room typically provides a sense of front and back, up and down. High ceilings draw attention upward, long aisles invite movement forward. Perfectly dimensioned rooms, however, provide no such orientation for a sense of movement or direction. The temple's inner sanctuary employed

---

15. Bloch-Smith, "'Who is the King of Glory?'" 26.

this innovative design principle to represent perfection and to suspend the imaginative worshiper in space and time within the eternal majesty of God. This ancient, biblical design was so remarkable that, millennia later, Renaissance "architects attempted to re-create the perfection of this lost archetype from which all the other orders were thought to be derived."[16] Here is an example of using knowledge to reimagine reality.

The two massive pillars that stood at the entrance also pioneered artistic innovations (1 Kgs 7:15–22). The capital atop the bronze pillars included intricate latticework and stylized pomegranates, which were capped off with lily-work designs. This complicated feat of engineering appeared at other buildings during the Solomonic period.[17] The pillar with a flowering capital is typically associated with the Doric, Ionic, and Corinthian pillars of Greece. However, Solomon predates architecture in Greece, and this design appears to be an Israelite innovation exported elsewhere.[18] In considering the architecture of the temple, biblical scholar Carol Meyer observes:

> This leaves Israel, with its reported construction of an extraordinary temple-palace complex in Jerusalem, as a trendsetter in the material world of its day. Ancient Israel is best known in postbiblical religious tradition for its spiritual and literary contributions, for its wisdom documents and prophetic calls for justice. But for one brief period in the millennium or so of its history it may have taken the lead in artistic creativity.[19]

For ancient Israel, cultural advance did not produce theological retreat. The extraordinary inventions and exquisite sense of proportion exhibited at the temple revealed a bold interaction with ancient Israel's intellectual milieu, seemingly not hampered by fear but marked by curiosity and creativity. This fourth building block toward a biblical theology of cultural interaction challenges God's people to be cultural leaders who reimagine the common tools of human vocations for divine purposes.

Architecture of Scripture

While our exploration has focused on the architecture of the temple, a brief consideration of the ways in which biblical literature interacts with pagan sources of knowledge affirms that the temple is not an aberration but a

---

16. Wittkower, "Principles of Pallidio's Architecture," 82.
17. Mazar, *Archaeology of the Land*, 383.
18. Meyers, "Kinship and Kingship," 251.
19. Meyers, "Kinship and Kingship," 256.

paradigm. Scripture itself is constructed in deep conversation with the broader culture and reveals the same variations of cultural interactions. Although the Apostle Paul made clear that the pagan mind was futile and darkened with respect to salvation (Rom 1:21), he quoted Greek thinkers as authorities in his preaching at Athens. The two citations in his message—"In him we live and move and have our being . . . for we are indeed his offspring" (Acts 17:28)—were originally made about Zeus, and yet, Paul applied them in his evangelistic message to the one true God. As biblical scholar Howard Marshall notes, "Paul was prepared to take over the glimmerings of truth in pagan philosophy about the nature of God."[20]

This ability to receive, refine, reject, and reimagine pagan sources appeared throughout the Old Testament. The Book of Proverbs cited the non-Israelite "sayings of Agur" (Prov 30) and the "sayings of King Lemuel" (Prov 31). Moreover, the "sayings of the wise" (Prov 22:17—24:34) match an Egyptian collection called the *Wisdom of Amenemope*. Biblical law in Exodus inherited and interacted with a legal tradition shared with the Old Babylonian "Code of Hammurabi," while the covenant structure of the book of Deuteronomy employed the political language and ideological structure of the Hittite vassal treaty to provide the template for God's covenant relationship with Israel.

Perhaps one of the most surprising examples of engaging with the ideological milieu of broader culture appeared in the quintessential biblical doctrine, namely, the gospel. For early Christians, the Roman Empire dominated the Mediterranean world. In an age without the internet or TV, Rome propagated its agenda through monuments and inscriptions. Its architecture advanced imperial purpose through the imposing use of monuments and public edicts, such as the *Priene Calendar Inscription*, which commemorated the birthday of Caesar:

> Since Providence, which has ordered all things and is deeply interested in our life, has set in most perfect order by giving us Augustus, who she filled with virtue that he might benefit humankind, sending him as a savior, both for us and for our descendants, that he might end war and arrange all things. . . . The birthday of the god Augustus was the beginning of the good tidings [gospel] for the world that came by reason of him.[21]

When Mark began his Gospel by saying: "*The beginning of the gospel of Jesus Christ, the Son of God,*" he appears to be utilizing the language found on this inscription (Mark 1:1 ESV, emphasis added). Mark and the Calendar

---

20. Marshall, *Acts*, 289.
21. Evans, "Mark's Incipit," 68–69.

Inscription share the terms "god," "beginning," and "gospel," and they associate those terms with the idea of incarnation, a savior, and the blessings of peace and order. Of course, the gospel of Jesus Christ clearly dethroned Caesar and his purported gospel. Compatible with our preliminary exploration of the temple, Mark displayed the panoply of reception, refinement, rejection, and reimagination of his cultural surroundings.

Reconstructing Evangelicalism

When my son graduated from high school, I was struck by what his teachers had asked of him. He studied calculus and physics; he wrote complex arguments about American history; he learned a second language and world geography. This public-school curriculum is repeated throughout our country. Many high school students are given complexity, while churches are far too content offering a flannelgraph Jesus, seeking simplicity out of concern to make faith accessible.

Our intellectual and ethical conundrums are profound. Today's technological advances, biomedical possibilities, racial turmoil, debates about climate change, and shifting views on sexuality are all matters of immense complexity. These challenges, and a myriad of others, are boiling over in the context of deep social discord. The discipleship of the mind toward culture is more a *way* to think rather than a *what* to think. In developing principles and practices of engagement, Christians should show the intellectual honesty and humility that we ask of others. We do not want skeptics to reject the faith based upon simplistic assessments about church history or Christian theology and informed by a few articles or conversations. Conversely, when engaging with non-Christian people and sources of knowledge, we need discernment to receive what is true, refine what is helpful, reject what is false, and reimagine what could and should be. This is not easy. And humans, even sanctified ones, devolve toward the easy.

James exhorts us to "be quick to listen, slow to speak and slow to become angry, because human anger does not produce the righteousness that God desires" (Jas 1:19–20 NIV). The disciplines of the mouth apply well to the disciplines of the mind. Instead of a whack-a-mole response to culture, the architecture of the temple and of Scripture provides a template for how "to repair the fracture between spiritual and rational knowledge" and "to resolve the tension between the demands of personal belief and the constraints of a secularized public square."[22]

---

22. Worthen, *Apostles of Reason*, 6.

Because of common grace and the image of God, it should not be surprising that the visual language and architectural conventions of the ancient Near East appeared in the temple or that Solomon collaborated with the Sidonians in this sacred effort. In our complex and contentious day, how can we collaborate with others in a shared pursuit of the good, true, and beautiful? When confronted with any number of critical theories, can we glean the good ideas even within a bad ideology? And when the time comes for us to be countercultural, are we doing so without being encrusted by layers of our own biases? What does it mean for us to refine or reimagine in such innovative and creative ways that the world would view Christians not as cultural laggards or cultural warriors, but as cultural creators and redeemers?

To answer these questions, our faith needs a catechesis of complexity. The simplicity of our gospel presentation enables us to communicate clearly and quickly about God's love, human sin, and Christ's redemption. But what enables the rapid growth of Evangelicalism at times constrains its deeper growth. A faith so simply explained is too often left simplistic. The luxury of thinking in a nuanced way about what and how we receive, refine, reject, or reimagine requires time and patience in the study of Scripture and of society. Discipleship in this manner requires resources, events, curated experiences, collaborative endeavors, networked friendships, and long-term programs that are responsive to the Holy Spirit and formative in the ways people live and learn.

With the conviction that the good news of Jesus is necessary for both eternal salvation and present human flourishing, we need a comprehensive gospel for our common life. Missiologist Lesslie Newbigin once proposed that "the gospel is public truth" and "to affirm the gospel as public truth is to invite acceptance of a new starting point for thought, the truth of which will be proved only in the course of a life of reflection and action which proves itself more adequate to the totality of human experience than its rivals."[23] This effort is not a matter of bludgeoning others into acquiescence but of building a life together with a deep sense of loyalty to others created in the image of God. The gospel as public truth works out and applies the Scriptures for the church within society as a whole and at a particular time.

The challenges facing Evangelicalism are real, but so are the opportunities. Should we write an obituary for its demise (as some would wish) or a birth announcement of its renewal?

---

23. Newbigin, "Gospel as Public Truth," 2.

PART TWO: OPPORTUNITIES

Conclusion

When I became president of the National Association of Evangelicals in 2020, both congratulations and condolences came my way. Many people wondered whether we needed a new name, but I am not yet ready to give up the term "evangelical." In November 2019, I joined eight hundred evangelical delegates from ninety different countries who met in Jakarta, Indonesia, at the World Evangelical Alliance. At a plenary session, the subject of American Evangelicalism was discussed by global leaders from Asia, Europe, Africa, and Latin America. Instead of leveling scathing critiques, our brothers and sisters exhorted American Evangelicals to work through our issues and to engage the rest of the world as partners in the work of the good news.

As I was processing the heavy call for the renewal of Christ followers in the US, I boarded the bus from the convention center to the hotel. I went to the back of the bus to join a jovial group whose laughter led me to assume they were from a fun country without problems. Turns out they were evangelical delegates from two sides of one of the most tragic and violent histories of conflict, with some of the most intractable challenges: Israel and Palestine. And there they were laughing and strategizing on how they would collaborate after the conference. Why would we wish to disassociate ourselves from these brothers and sisters? How American would it be for us to ditch a term simply because it is inconvenient for us? Instead of getting lost in whack-a-mole battles, we are invited to be a generative part of God's mission around the world. May the depth of history and the breadth of God's global work help us to reconstruct an Evangelicalism worthy of the good news of Jesus Christ.

Bibliography

Ackerman, Joshua M., Christopher C. Nocera, and John A. Bargh. "Incidental Haptic Sensations Influence Social Judgments and Decisions." *Science* 328.5968 (2010) 1712–15.

Barzun, Jacques. *From Dawn to Decadence: 500 Years of Western Cultural Life—1500 to the Present.* New York: HarperCollins, 2000.

Bebbington, D. W. *Evangelicalism in Modern Britain: A History from the 1730s to the 1980s.* London: Routledge, 1989.

Bloch-Smith, Elizabeth. "'Who Is the King of Glory?' Solomon's Temple and Its Symbolism." In *Scripture and Other Artifacts: Essays on the Bible and Archaeology in Honor of Philip J. King*, edited by Michael D. Coogan, J. Cheryl Exum, and Lawrence Stager, 18–31. Louisville: Westminster John Knox, 1994.

Cogan, Mordechai. *1 Kings: A New Translation with Introduction and Commentary.* Anchor Bible 10. New York: Doubleday, 2001.

Evans, Craig A. "Mark's Incipit and the Priene Calendar Inscription: From Jewish Gospel to Greco-Roman Gospel." *Journal of Greco-Roman Christianity and Judaism* 1 (2000) 67–81.

Goldhagen, Sarah Williams. *Welcome to Your World.* New York: Harper, 2017.

Gutheim, Frederick, ed. *Frank Lloyd Wright on Architecture: Selected Writings (1894–1940).* New York: Grosset's Universal Library, 1941.

Hurowitz, Victor. *I Have Built You an Exalted House: Temple Building in the Bible in Light of Mesopotamian and North-West Semitic Writings.* Journal for the Study of the Old Testament Supplement Series. Edited by David J. A. Clines and Philip R. Davies. Sheffield: JSOT, 1992.

King, Philip J., and Lawrence E. Stager. *Life in Biblical Israel.* Library of Ancient Israel. Louisville: Westminster John Knox, 2001.

Marshall, I. Howard. *Acts: An Introduction and Commentary.* Tyndale New Testament Commentaries. Downers Grove, IL: IVP Academic, 2008.

Mazar, Amihai. *Archaeology of the Land of the Bible 10,000–586 B.C.E.* The Anchor Bible Reference Library. New York: Doubleday, 1992.

Meyers, Carol L. "Kinship and Kingship: The Early Monarchy." In *The Oxford History of the Biblical World*, edited by Michael D. Coogan, 221–71. Oxford: Oxford University Press, 1998.

Mierse, William E. *Temples and Sanctuaries from the Early Iron Age Levant: Recovery after Collapse.* History, Archaeology, and Culture of the Levant. Edited by Jeffrey A. Blakely and K. Lawson Younger. Winona Lake, IN: Eisenbrauns, 2012.

Newbigin, Lesslie. "The Gospel as Public Truth." *Touchstone* 5.3 (1992) 1–3.

Tarler, David, and Jane M. Cahill. "David, City of." In *The Anchor Bible Dictionary*, edited by David Noel Freedman, 52–67. New Haven: Yale University Press, 1992.

Taylor, Charles. *A Secular Age.* Cambridge, MA: Belknap, 2007.

Wittkower, Rudolf. "Principles of Pallidio's Architecture." *Journal of the Warburg and Courtauld Institutes* 8 (1945) 68–106.

Worthen, Molly. *Apostles of Reason: The Crisis of Authority in American Evangelicalism.* New York: Oxford University Press, 2014.

Index

activism, 9, 25, 79, 98, 127, 129, 141
Aladura movement, 59, 63
American Evangelicalism, xiv, 7, 75, 102–4, 106, 110, 112, 114, 122, 135
apocalypse, 7, 50
Aquinas, Thomas. *See* Thomas Aquinas.
Assemblies of God, 60, 63
Association of Evangelicals in Africa (AEA), 57–58
Assyrian Church of the East, 124
Augustine, 6–7, 118–20, 122
authority, 10, 12, 31, 36, 57, 85, 127, 145
Azusa Street Revival, 60, 64

Bababola, Aye, 59
Barber, William J., II, 20
Barth, Karl, 26, 28, 73
Barzun, Jacques, 140
Bavinck, Herman, 90–100
beatific vision, 111–12
Beaumont, Susan, 89
Bebbington Quadilateral, 9, 58, 127, 129, 141
Bennett, Dennis J., 62
biblicism. *See* Bebbington Quadrilateral.
Black Lives Matter, 141
Bonhoeffer, Dietrich, 20, 81, 120
Braide, Sokari, 59

Calvinism, 91
Canterbury Tales, The, 3–4, 10
Celestial Church of Christ, 64
charismatic, 59–65, 126, 129
Chaucer, Geoffrey, 3–4, 10
cherubim, 144–45
Cherubim and Seraphim Movement, 64
Christ Apostolic Church, 64
Christian Nationalism, 16–20, 23, 107–8
Christian Union (CU), 60, 64
Church Growth movement, 103
church planting movements, 103
civil reconciliation, 20–21, 24
civil religion, 88
classism, 39
colonialism, 31
conversion, 58, 63, 65, 104–6, 127, 132, 135, 137
conversionism. *See* Bebbington Quadrilateral.
COVID-19, 23, 27
crucicentrism. *See* Bebbington Quadrilateral.
culture, xiii, 5–6, 8, 11, 13, 40, 43–44, 50, 53, 60, 62, 65, 67, 75, 78, 89, 93, 99, 102, 105–8, 110–12, 114, 117, 123, 139–42, 147–48

David, 45, 120
deconstruction, xiii–xiv, 50, 117, 122–24

INDEX

dissociation, 102, 106–13
dissociative public discourse, 107
diversity, 17, 30, 128

Eastern Orthodox, 124
Edwards, Jonathan, 56
Ejiwumi, Theophilus O., 60
Elton, Pa S. G., 63–64
enthymematic persuasion, 104
eschatology, 34, 75, 78, 83, 85, 123, 141
Evangelical Fellowship in Anglican
    Communion (EFAC), 64

Fellowship of Christian Students (FCS),
    64
Foursquare Gospel Church, 60
Fox, George, 56
Full Gospel Business Fellowship
    (FGBMFI), 64
fundamentalist, 122, 128

gnosticism, 36
Graham, Billy, 51, 56
Graham, Michael, 129
Great Awakening, 13, 55–56, 128
Gregory of Nyssa, 119–20

Hiebert, Paul, 67
Holy Spirit, the, 13, 31, 33, 57, 59, 62, 64,
    76, 79, 83, 86, 113, 120–21, 124,
    127, 133, 135, 149
Hour of Freedom, 60, 63
humility, 31–32, 66, 123–24, 148
Hybels, Bill, 104
hypersexualized, 50–51

Ibiam, Francis Akanu, 60
Idahosa, Benson, 60, 63
idolatry, 37, 52, 63
image of God, 32, 34, 37, 119–20, 149
imagination, 5, 8–9, 10, 12–13, 32–33, 42,
    79, 85, 90, 97–100, 124, 140, 147
incentive structures, 105–6
Intercession for Africa, 64
inventio, 113

Jesus, 7, 9–12, 19–22, 24–28, 30, 32–35,
    38–40, 45, 48–49, 52, 58, 65–66,
    75, 77, 82, 85, 94–95, 99–100,
    110–12, 120, 125, 127, 129, 131,
    139, 141, 148–50
Jim Crow, 33

King, Martin Luther, Jr., 20, 25
kingdom of God, 52, 65, 86, 95, 97, 120
kingdom-at-hand, 20, 25, 27
kingdom-to-come, 20, 26, 27
Kuyper, Abraham, 91, 95

liminal space, liminality, 89–90, 98–99
Luther, Martin, 4

Mandela, Nelson, 23–24
manhood, 45, 49–50
McGavran, Donald, 103
McGrath, Alister, 127–29
meritocracy, 39
metatheology, 67
Methodism, 133–34, 136–37
Misión Integral, 36
mission (of the church), 40, 57, 60, 66,
    68, 82, 102–14, 130, 139
modernism, 107
Moore, Russell, 35, 50
munus triplex, 94

Neo-Calvinism, 91
New Independent Pentecostal Churches
    (NPCs), 64
Newbigin, Lesslie, 149
Niemöller, Martin, 120

Obama, Barack, 19, 116–17, 121
Ockenga, Harold, 56
Oriental Orthodox Church, 124
Orimolade, Moses, 59
otherism, 23

Parham, Charles Fox, 59, 64
paternalism, 68
patriarchy, 39, 124
Pentecostalism, 59–60, 62
Pope Leo X, 4

INDEX

prophetic preaching, 26–28
Protestant Reformation, 3–5, 8, 12, 128
Puritans, 10

race, 37, 96
reconciliation, 17, 19–24, 26, 28, 33, 35, 78, 83, 136
reconstruction, xiv, 30–32, 36, 40, 116–18, 120–24, 137, 140, 142
replacement theory, 17–18, 28
revivalism. *See* Bebbington Quadrilateral.
Roberts, Bill, 63
Roman Catholic, 59, 124, 129

salvific reconciliation, 20–21
Scripture Union (SU), 60–61
social reconciliation, 19–24
sola scriptura, 84–85
Solzhenitsyn, Aleksandr, 124–25
Student Christian Movement (SCM), 60

Tanner, Kathryn, 108
Taylor, Charles, 6, 44, 89, 140
temple, 40, 140–46, 148–49

Thomas Aquinas, 111, 118, 119–20
Torah, 21
Trinitarian, 83, 127
triune (God), 76, 80, 82–83, 96–98, 133, 135
Trump, Donald, 8, 19, 23, 35, 66, 69, 109
Tutu, Desmond, 23

van Gennop, Arnold, 89
Vivian, Bradford, 108
Voting Rights Act of 1965, 23

Wells, David, 84
Wesley, John, 55–56, 130–37
white Evangelicals, 35, 66, 109, 124
white supremacy, 18, 34
Whitefield, George, 56
woke Evangelical, 107–10
Women Aglow, 64
World Action Team for Christ, 62

xenophobia, 28

Zinzendorf, Nicolaus, 55–56

www.ingramcontent.com/pod-product-compliance
Lightning Source LLC
Chambersburg PA
CBHW030858170426
43193CB00009BA/649